The London Underground

Surface Stock Planbook
1863-1959

AN HUNTLEY

LONDON
IAN ALLAN LTD

Contents

Preface

First published 1988

ISBN 0 7110 1721 2

© Ian Huntley 1988

Published by Ian Allan Ltd, Shepperton, Surrey; and printed by Ian Allan Printing Ltd at their works at Coombelands in Runnymede, England

Front cover:
Red liveried 'Q' stock leaves Surrey Docks station on the East London line in August 1970. *Colour-Rail (LT8)*

Rear cover, top:
Class E 0-4-4T No L44 in maroon livery at Neasden shed in May 1961.
J. H. L. Adams/Colour-Rail (LT21)

Rear cover, bottom:
Electric locomotive No 7 *Edmund Burke* enters Baker Street with compartment stock in tow in 1959.
J. G. Dewing/Colour-Rail (LT6)

Production limitations have made it necessary to restrict the coverage of this volume to stock which ran between 1863 and 1959. Although classed as 'underground' stock, these locomotives and cars were all built to a loading gauge similar, but not identical to that of main line railways*, but ran in sub-surface cuttings, underground sections and tunnels. Later, of course, the Metropolitan had an extensive 'Main Line' surface section.

As initially constructed there were only three tunnels, one the 728yd Clerkenwell tunnel of the original Metropolitan line. The second is the deeper 733yd 'widened line' tunnel parallel to the Clerkenwell tunnel, and the third, the Campden Hill tunnel of 421yd.

A rough idea of the extent of the sub-surface workings can be judged in that the Inner Circle had a total length of 13 miles 8 chains, of which 2 miles were laid with two sets of double track. Minimum radius on the Circle was 10 chains, although the spur connec-tions of the GNR line was down to 6 chains (one chain being 66ft). Various spurs and extensions gradually extended these workings.

Locomotives and Stock are depicted in original, or early service form as far as possible, for it must be appreciated that stock constructed towards the latter end of the period survived many expansion programmes and modifi-cations both in equipments and livery, and were not finally withdrawn until the early 1960s.

In common with all other UK rail-ways both the MET and the MDR originally offered three classes of accommodation. However, the MET withdrew all Second Class accommo-dation on 17 December 1906, converting most of it to Third Class. MDR steam stock maintained First, Second and Third Class accommodation until the advent of electrification in July 1905. Thereafter, First and Third Classes were continued into the London Trans-port era, with the first withdrawal of First Class accommodation occurring during 1941.

* 'Metrogauge' restricted the overall length of vehicles to a maximum of 57ft and the height to 12ft 8in for stock working over the underground lines and tunnel sections of the Metropolitan Railway.

Acknowledgement
My thanks to Graeme Bruce for his assistance during the production of this book.

Introduction

The underground railways of London are over 120 years old and like a lot of subjects of great age, their early beginnings were not recorded on film, but were left to the artist, engraver and lithographer to portray as best they could. Thus, in most cases details of locomotives and stock of the 1860s and 1870s shown in engravings appear far too vague and ethereal to give even a hint of reality. Add to that the fact that such engineering elevations as there were did not come before the public eye, and it can be seen that three-dimensional impressions were, therefore, hard to form with any certainty. Inevitably, with the passage of time many of the unseen builders' drawings have become lost forever. This has produced the sad result that modern historical accounts of London's underground equipments usually pass lightly over the first important 40 years, with but a few words accompanied only by the reproduction of old engravings.

This situation is in strong contrast to the position concerning the modern stock of today where prolific use of the camera, colour reproduction and detailed engineering elevations, enables the reader to gather an instant three-dimensional impression of an underground car without leaving his armchair. One aim of this book has been to put engineering drawings in the place of the artists' impressions and engravings of the very early locomotives and rolling stock that appeared when the Metropolitan Railway came into being in 1863, and to continue with drawings of subsequent items of hardware that have never been seen in this form before. It is hoped that these pioneer outlines may serve to hasten the appearance of further, more precise details of these interesting artifacts of public transport.

This reference has been based upon three generations of family interest in London's underground railway system. Probably started circa 1880, the first book of notes was completed and dated August 1883. Further notes have continued right up to the present day. All of the material combined to form a large skeletal outline which looked informative and impressive, but initial uncertainty as to the degree to which its accuracy could be relied upon, raised doubts as to the wisdom of putting it into book form. However, when more modern research compilations were examined it was found that numerical sequences fitted parts of the skeleton. Also, printed descriptions of stock could be fitted to actual sketches and dimensioned drawings made decades ago — a situation which began to make further work seem worthwhile. In addition, the Engineering and Public Relations Department of London Underground Limited were able to supply data and drawing prints which confirmed the all important dimensions and references to stock numbering.

Had it not been for the stimulation provided by these very interested persons, their organisations and societies and the published material that has appeared on the pages of railway and engineering magazines, this present work might not have come into being.

What the underground following have been lacking were engineering elevations to a modern standard and the author/draughtsman can take no more credit than that for taking the work of so many individuals (including relatives) and recasting some of it into drawings and notes covering some of the locomotives and rolling stock of the chosen period.

Ian Huntley
Stoke Poges, 1987

Abbreviations

Railway Companies:

C&SLR	City & South London Railway
CLR	Central London Railway
GCR	Great Central Railway
GNR	Great Northern Railway
GWR	Great Western Railway
H&CR	Hammersmith & City Railway
LBSCR	London, Brighton & South Coast Railway
LCDR	London, Chatham & Dover Railway
LNWR	London & North Western Railway
LPTB	London Passenger Transport Board
LTSR	London, Tilbury & Southend Railway
MDR	Metropolitan District Railway
MET	Metropolitan Railway
MR	Midland Railway
SECR	South Eastern & Chatham Railway

Manufacturers:

Brush	Brush Electrical Engineering Co and its forebears
BT-H	British Thomson-Houston Co
BWE	British Westinghouse Electrical and Manufacturing Co (later Metropolitan-Vickers Electrical Co)
GEC	General Electric Co
Met-Cam	Metropolitan-Cammell Ltd and its forebears, Metropolitan Carriage and Cammell Laird amalgamated to become Metropolitan Cammell in 1929

Hauled Stock:

1	First Class Car
2	Second Class Car
3	Third Class Car
B2	Brake Second
B3	Brake Third
1/2	First/Second Class Composite
1/3	First/Third Class Composite

Electric Stock:

M	Motor Car
ME	End Motor Car
MM	Middle Motor Car
3M	Third Class Motor Car
DM	Double-Equipped Motor Car
SM	Single-Equipped Motor Car
T	Trailer
3T	Third Class Trailer
1/3	First/Third Class Composite Trailer
CT	Control Trailer
DT	Driving Trailer
1DT	First Class Driving Trailer
1/3CT	First/Third Class Composite Control Trailer
1T	First Class Trailer
2T	Second Class Trailer
B2T	Brake Second Trailer
B3T	Brake Third Trailer

Gooch 'Metropolitan' 2-4-0T 1862

The Metropolitan Railway had commenced investigations into a 'smokeless' locomotive design as early as 1856; but the whole idea of running steam engines in an underground environment was then revolutionary. Nevertheless, it was possible, 'provided the sulphurous fumes from combustion could be all but eliminated, and exhaust steam turned back into water'. The company's Chief Engineer, John Fowler, had proved the practical possibilities of a 'smokeless condenser locomotive' with the trials of his 2-4-0 tender engine (built by Robert Stephenson & Co as works No 1314) between November 1861 and August 1862, on newly laid MET tracks. However, the MET's first steam locomotive revealed a number of design faults relating to its firebox, adjoining brick chamber and water consenser. Stephenson's suggested remedy of building an entirely new and unorthodox design found little favour, largely due to the expense involved, and Fowler redirected his enquiries towards Beyer Peacock. However, late in November 1861 a hastily drawn up agreement was reached with GWR for the provision of locomotives and stock and the operation of the services which were expected to start late in the following year.

Thus to Daniel Gooch fell the onerous task of designing the world's first 'condensing' underground locomotive.

Below:

A very familiar lithograph impression of a broad gauge train of three carriages passing over the Praed Street Junction on its way from Edgware Road to Bishops Road (Paddington GWR station). The locomotive depicted is the Vulcan Foundry-built *Hornet* and is shown with a cast rectangular name plate on the forward part of the boiler in a similar position to that adopted by the later MET 4-4-0T locomotives. *(22456)*

Right:

A contemporary artist's impression of King's Cross Metropolitan Railway station shortly after the opening showing an original GWR-designed broad gauge locomotive and coaching stock in operation. From the meticulous detail that has gone into the painting of the station structure, it would appear that the artist made use of photographic reference. Unfortunately the same cannot be said about the locomotive and carriages. *(H4192)*

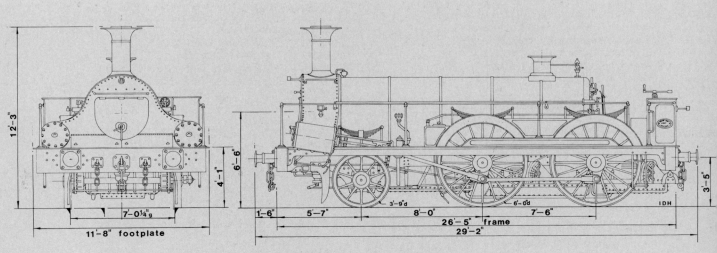

It was a 2-4-0 well tank, some 29ft in length over the buffers having 6ft coupled wheels, with 16in×24in outside cylinders. The latter layout was then unusual but it enabled pipes between smokebox and cylinders to carry diverted exhaust steam back into a condensing tank carried beneath the footplate and boiler.

These locomotives, without weatherboards 'lest anything should obscure the driver's vision', must have looked a splendid sight emerging from tunnels, where an open firebox door 'caused a bright yellow glow like an approaching firefly' as *Punch* described it. With special baffles within the firebox, coke combustion was near enough complete, but unfortunately the short condensing pipe runs lost little heat and the feed water soon boiled. Hot water was frequently exchanged for cold, but even so it was often necessary to exhaust steam in the normal way, which caused inconvenience to both the passengers and the service.

In all 22 of the class were built — six each by Vulcan Foundry and Kitson & Co, the remainder at Swindon Works, and it was these locomotives that commenced the Metropolitan service on Monday 10 January 1863. They ceased working the MET services on Monday 10 August 1863, but continued to work the through GWR services over the underground lines until Monday 15 March 1869, when all broad gauge workings ceased.

Specification:

Inside plate framed, domeless, well tank. Two outside cylinders 16in×24in. Fitted with the world's first condensing apparatus (a deflecting valve mounted at the bottom of the blastpipe).

Heating area: Tubes 615sq ft, firebox 125sq ft, total 740sq ft.

Grate area: 18.5sq ft.

Boiler pressure: 100lb/sq in.

Tractive effort: 11,500lb approximately.

Water capacity: 375gal, with a 422gal condensing tank, total 797gal.

Coke capacity: 16cwt.

Brake type: Steam.

Stock numbering:

All of the group received nameplates as follows:

Builder	Year	Name	Works No	Name	Works No	
Vulcan Foundry	1862	*Hornet*	484	*Wasp*	487	
Vulcan Foundry	1862	*Bee*	485	*Mosquito*	488	
Vulcan Foundry	1862	*Gnat*	486	*Locust*	489	Operated MET
Kitson & Co	1862	*Shah*	976	*Mogul*	979	services
Kitson & Co	1862	*Bey*	977	*Kaiser*	980	
Kitson & Co	1862	*Czar*	978	*Khan*	981	
GWR (Swindon)		*Fleur-de-Lys*	*	*Azalia*	*	
1863-64		*Rose*	*	*Lily*	*	Operated GWR
		Thistle	*	*Myrtle*	*	services over
		Shamrock	*	*Violet*	*	the MET lines
		Camelia	*	*Laurel*	*	

* Believed to be in the 100 series.

Livery:

GWR green boiler cladding and bunker, fine lined in gilt with boiler bands black with fine gilt edge lining. The frames, brass edged splashers, wheels and footplate valance indian red. Smokebox, cylinder cladding and polished copper-capped chimney, black. Safety valve casing, smokebox/boiler cladding and various fittings polished brass. Polished steel coupling and connecting rods, slide bars, cylinder end covers and handrails. Initially no actual reference to ownership was marked.

Brown, Marshalls Eight-Wheel Stock 1862

The original eight-wheel rigid coaches, designed by the GWR for the opening of the MET were a great advance over the more common four- or six-wheel stock found elsewhere. Such broad gauge magnificence complete with brilliant town gas lighting was to instantly dispel any fear of travel underground, or so it was hoped for the majority of passengers.

In 1852 the GWR had built six, eight-wheel non-bogie coaches for main line use, which vastly improved passenger comfort at speed. Dubbed 'Long Charleys', they were withdrawn during 1862, and then served as the prototypes for the proposed MET coach stock. After suitable modification these cars also ran on the MET. At the same time drawings for the new stock were

passed to Brown, Marshalls & Co together with an order for 39 coaches, having a length over buffers of some 42ft, running on 3ft 3in spoked wheels.

Gas was stored in top-weighted bags placed in a continuous box mounted on the roof. Each pair of bags shared an indicator equipped with double pointers, each of which rose and fell with the amount of gas between 'full' and 'empty', the latter condition being indicated by the letters 'F' and 'E'. To fill the bags, town gas was taken from a trackside hydrant through a valve set in

Above:

A trial trip on the Underground on the opening day. Here an artist has depicted a broad gauge train of three or four rigid eight-wheeled carriages together with six specially fitted out low-sided wagons tacked on to the rear — a picture impossible to capture using a camera. Fortunately, photographs of the latter wagons and engineering drawings of both carriages and locomotives do exist so that an authentic scene could be portrayed with the modern camera of today, using scale models.
(22567)

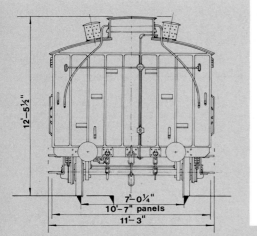

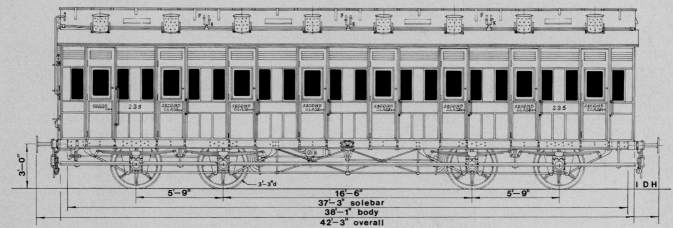

Above:

The first public train from Bishops Road as depicted by a contemporary artist, trying to capture the scene as it was on 10 January 1863. Unfortunately it was difficult to put such an image on a photographic plate and the real impression of broad gauge carriages, with gas bag boxes and lamp tops on the roof areas has been lost to us. *(23029)*

a 'main' running beneath each car, and up an end bulkhead to run along the roof feeding each bag. Outlet spurs connected bags to lamps, initially with two lamps for each compartment but later two lamps were placed above each partition, the light being shared in adjacent compartments.

With an internal car width of just under 10ft, even a seven-a-side Third Class compartment was roomy. Thus, First Class at five-a-side was sumptuous. Three body styles were built — one each for First, Second and Third Classes, with a fourth style having composite First and Second Class accommodation. As a non-bogied stock, the outermost axles had side play in the axleguard for negotiating any curve, and no attempt was made to provide a radial or swinging movement.

The only brakes provided were Fay and Newall's 'hand break' system fitted in the end compartment of each end car of a train. Operated by the guard, only the inner pair of wheels were braked with a single wooden block each. The compartment was shared with passengers, and the brake wheel and rodding took up the space of one seat.

NB: With the withdrawal of the GWR stock, the MET commissioned Ashbury to construct very similar vehicles but for standard gauge use.

Specification:

Iron underframe with composite components. Hardwood framing and body panels in a perpendicular style. Plain arc roof of canvas-covered boards topped with a 'gasbox'. Rigid non-bogie running gear, with standard coupling and buffing gear. Individual upper footboards; full length lower footboards.

Compartments: Either six Firsts, eight Seconds, eight Thirds or (Composite) three Firsts, flanked at each end by two Seconds. First Class compartments featured four folding armrests per side, with sprung upholstery in quality braided cloth, window curtains and a floor carpet. Second Class compartments were fitted with padded cloth seats and backrests, and linoleum floor. Third Class, plain varnished seat boards and interior.

Marshalling: Generally B3-1/2-1-B2 or B3-1/2-B2.

Stock numbering:

On paper, the MET gave the new cars Nos 1-39 and the converted 'Long Charleys' Nos 40-45.

	1	1/2	2 or B2	3 or B3	'Long Charleys'
MET (Ledger entry)	1-6	7-15	16-25	26-39	40-45
GWR	226-271	272-280	231-240	102-115	(unknown)

Livery:

Plain clear varnished teak, with white enamelled panelling above the waist (the white upper sides restricted to First Class only by 1868). White lead roof canvas. Finely lettered with class in two lines, and numbered in gilt, possibly fine black lined, with white and blue blocking. All underframe and running gear was a flat dark grey. Wheels were black with polished steel tyre edges. The footboards were light grey. No actual reference to ownership was marked.

Twin Carriage 1869

Unfair criticism was often made of the eight-wheel rigid stock*, mainly with reference to their riding characteristics. True, they were very solid and heavy, and thus Francis Burnett investigated an experimental composite twin carriage comprising a three-compartment First Class vehicle, and a four-compartment Second Class companion — both four-wheeled units being closely coupled with a semi-permanent central attachment but having conventional buffers and draw-gear at the outer ends.

This new vehicle, which was fractionally longer than its rigid counterpart, was quite successful during initial trials, so an order for 24 similar vehicles was placed with the Oldbury Carriage Co for 11 First, nine Second and four Third Class cars.

All these cars followed very much the same style of construction and had town gas (gasbox) lighting, though all-round economies in weight saving cut down the number of burners in all but the First Class cars. Second and Third Class compartments had only one lamp above each position for each pair of compartments, the lamps being positioned on alternate sides along the lengths of the car. However, they introduced top lights into true MET stock for the first time, and a slight improvement in general comfort, though plain boards and waist-high partitioning remained with Third Class cars.

The new stock was subject to various modifications and perhaps for that reason ran mostly on the service to St Johns Wood. Changes were made in braking, for example, first employing Clark's chain brake which embraced brakes on all coaches, and later Smith's simple vacuum form. Later still the lighting was changed to the Pintsch

Below:

Few photographs seem to exist of MET 'Twin-coach' stock. Short-lived, the coupled pairs were soon separated and were later run with normal buffing gear as individual items of stock; this would appear to be the situation shown here at Pinner on Monday 25 May 1885 when the first MET train left for Baker Street. The locomotive is alleged to be Class A 4-4-0T No 65 or 66. The coaches have been updated with the provision of oil-gas lighting and have the vacuum brake. *(22091)*

high pressure system, and some reports suggest one twin unit (possibly the prototype) was fitted with round-topped doors for trials purposes, whilst running in tunnel sections and between Gloucester Road and the spur terminal of West Brompton.

Initially run as four twin units per train, they were later reported to run as an additional twin unit with rigid stock. Later they appear to have been separated and rebuffered at their inner ends to run singly within rigid sets. Many lessons were learned from the use of these carriages which set new standards for incorporation in subsequent stock designs.

* This includes the standard gauge cars built for the MET (which superseded the GWR broad gauge stock) and which formed the bulk of passenger vehicles until the advent of the later 'Bogie' stock.

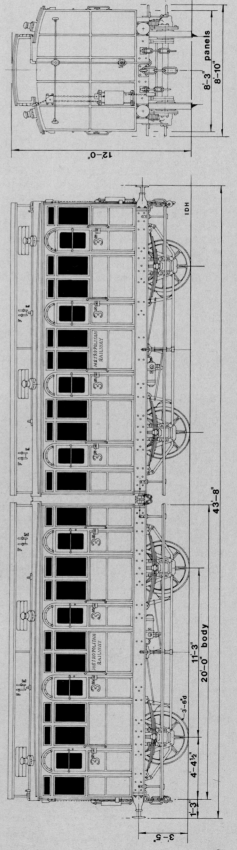

Specification:

Iron underframe. Hard wood framed and panelled body. Plain arc roof of canvas-covered boards, topped with the 'gasbox'. Rigid four-wheel running gear, close-coupled in semi-permanent pairs. Standard buffing and drawgear at outer ends. Clark's chain brake fitted when introduced, later changed to Smith's simple vacuum brake. Full-length double footboards.

Compartments: Three individual body styles, featuring either three Firsts, four Seconds or four Thirds. First Class with four-a-side, well sprung and upholstered seating, with less padding for Second Class and bare varnished boards in Third Class.

Marshalling: Original formation B2-1-3-3B, or similar.

Stock numbering:

Builder	Year	1	2	3
Oldbury	1869	141/143, 158-168	142/144, 149-157	145, 146-148

Livery:

Plain varnished teak for all but First Class, the latter with white panelling above the waist. White lead roof canvas. Finely lettered with owning company and class, each in two lines, and numbered in gilt, with white and blue blocking. All underframe and running gear flat dark grey. Wheels black with white-painted tyre edges. Light grey footboards.

Beyer Peacock 4-4-0T (Metropolitan Railway) 1864

It had always been the aim of the MET to own its locomotives and rolling stock, but there were a lot of problems to be overcome.

The Manchester-based locomotive builders of Beyer Peacock & Co probably received their first preliminary enquiries for a small number of engines for the MET at some time early in 1862, and perhaps again in late January 1863. Following the emergency of August 1863 when a dispute with the GWR resulted in the withdrawal of all the

Below:
MET Class A locomotive No 18 *Hercules* **(Works No 429)** after some time in service. It still had wooden brake blocks, but not yet the vacuum brake. Painted mainly green, the tanks and bunker are lined out in numerous panels of broad black banding thinly edged in straw. Boiler banding is unlined, and the dome appears to be painted in the same olive green. This livery differs greatly from the original form of August 1864. *Ian Allan Library*

Top right:
MET Class A 4-4-0T No 18 *Hercules* again — this time in a very early green livery, in which only the tank sides are lined out in three panels. The lining appears to be of broad straw form, thinly edged in black above and to the left, and in ivory below and to the right. The dome appears to be of polished brass. *Ian Allan Library*

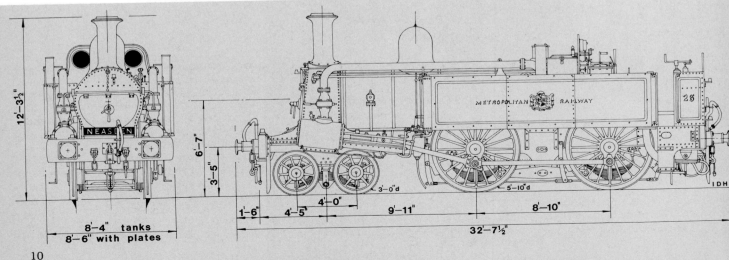

Left:
This photograph, taken at Hammersmith around 1868, shows No 4 carrying a white disc on the buffer beam. The train is formed of a four-car set of eight-wheel rigid stock of early 1864-66 vintage, having square-topped doors, and with the town-gas lighting boxes on the roof-tops. The third car is a First Class vehicle, as indicated by its white painted upper panelling. *(H/8258)*

latter's motive power and stock from MET service, and once locomotives loaned by the GNR had settled into running the services, it was then time for John Fowler to reconsider an updated specification for a locomotive that could be equally happy operating on a surface main line, as underground.

Whatever details Fowler prescribed it was up to Beyer Peacock to produce the final answer, which included a highly efficient condensing system; and as that company already had produced a number of tank engine designs capable of being adapted and expanded for other railways, the MET requirement did not present too many problems, and the design soon crystalised into a 4-4-0T form.

Inclined 17¼in×24in outside cylinders and 5ft 9in coupled wheels, spread over a generous wheelbase which included a four-wheel Bissell truck enabling smooth running under most track conditions, formed the basis of a well thought out and handsome design of some 31ft 7½in overall length. The later extension of the bunker increased the latter by 1ft as indicated in the drawing.

With an initial order for 18 locomotives the first completed engine was delivered to the MET and commenced trials in June 1864. Although the basic design proved effective and capable of further development, by 1865 it was apparent that it did not provide the ultimate solution to underground motive power requirements.

Specification:

Inside framed, side tank locomotive, with two inclined outside cylinders 17¼in×24in, fitted with condensing apparatus.

Heating area: Tubes 909sq ft, firebox 103sq ft, total 1,012sq ft.
Grate area: 19sq ft.
Boiler pressure: 120/130lb/sq in (later 160lb/sq in).
Tractive effort: 12,680lb approximately.
Water capacity: 1,000gal.
Coke capacity: 1ton 4cwt (later 1ton 10cwt).
Brake type: Steam (later vacuum).

Stock numbering (A class):

Builder	Year	MET No	Name	Works No	MET No	Name	Works No
Beyer Peacock	1864	1	*Jupiter*	412	11	*Latona*	422
Beyer Peacock	1864	2	*Mars*	413	12	*Cyclops*	423
Beyer Peacock	1864	3	*Juno*	414	13	*Daphne*	424
Beyer Peacock	1864	4	*Mercury*	415	14	*Dido*	425
Beyer Peacock	1864	5	*Apollo*	416	15	*Aurora*	426
Beyer Peacock	1864	6	*Medusa*	417	16	*Achilles*	427
Beyer Peacock	1864	7	*Orion*	418	17	*Ixion*	428
Beyer Peacock	1864	9	*Minerva*	419	18	*Hercules*	429
Beyer Peacock	1864	10	*Cerberus*	421	—	—	—
Beyer Peacock	1866	19-23	—	706-10			
Beyer Peacock	1868	24-28	–	770-74			
Beyer Peacock	1869	29-33	—	853-57			
Beyer Peacock	1869	39-44	—	863-68			
Beyer Peacock	1870	45-49	—	893-97			

Livery:

The original colour was bright olive green, panelled out with broad gilt lining finely edged with black on tank and bunker sides. Boiler, cylinder cladding and wheels also green, the latter with a fine chrome yellow line around the inner edge of the tyres. Boiler banding gilt finely edged in black. Chimney cap and condenser pipes polished copper, and dome cover bright brass. Buffer beam front and end faces vermilion, edged in black divided by fine chrome yellow lining. Cylinder end covers, slide bars, connecting and coupling rods, buffer heads and shanks, handrailing and various other fittings polished steel. Chimney, smokebox and running plate black. Polished cut-out brass numerals on front of chimney. Frames and other detail below the footplate in flat dark grey. From 1885 the basic colour was changed to dark chocolate (crimson lake) with black lining edged with chrome yellow. The dome covers were painted in crimson lake. There were several schemes of panelling, lining and lettering. Initially no actual reference to ownership was marked.

District 4-4-0T 1871

In 1871 the District ordered 24 locomotives from Beyer Peacock of similar design to those built for the Metropolitan but with minor detail differences. Later batches differed from the original batch. On some, overall cabs were fitted, but they were subsequently removed and plain weatherboarding front and rear was introduced. Later still the front board was extended back at an angle to provide stowage for destination plates.

The early Bissell truck was replaced by the Adams bogie in the second batch, and retrospective modification was carried out on the earlier batch. From 1875 the adoption of the Westinghouse brake required the mounting of a brake

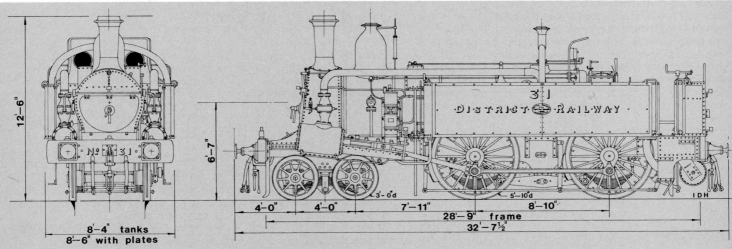

Far left:

MDR 4-4-0T No 36 (Works No 2058), the last of the third batch, in photographic grey in February 1881. The Westinghouse brake pump and reservoir have been added. This was the last of type to be built with the bell-mouthed dome cover and Salter spring-balanced safety valves. Nos 31-36 were fitted with built-up GN-type chimneys. Cast iron brake blocks are employed, with plain, unfluted coupling rods. *LPC (8230)*

Left:

An interesting view of **MDR 4-4-0T No 10** at the West Brompton terminus in May 1876, still in the original livery. A green (or red)-centred, white-edged LSWR-style disc is carried on the central lamp bracket of the buffer beam. The four-coach train of four-wheeled stock has oil 'pot lamp' lighting, and round-topped doors. The end of the leading coach is fitted out for use by the guard. *(U4650)*

Above:

MDR No 53, seen in later life, has a plain chimney and dome and is unlined with plain unblocked lettering. Coke is no longer in use as large cobbles of coal are piled up in the bunker. Note the fluted coupling rod. The picture is probably dated around the turn of the century. *G. Spiller*

pump on the left-hand side ahead of the tank, and an air cylinder below the bunker. Chimney styles also varied from batch to batch, as did boiler construction which could be of either iron or steel.

In order to avoid confusion with the MET locomotives the first 24 were lettered rather than numbered. However, from the second batch, the whole fleet was returned to normal numbering. Internal differences showed there were 164 tubes as opposed to 166 on the MET locomotives, and the external length of the firebox was 5ft 7in (approximately 1ft shorter), thus giving 3sq ft less grate area.

Like their MET counterparts, all went through repeated stages of repair and reboilering, with changes in chimney style and other fittings. Such changes were often accompanied by a change in livery as well. All early locomotives initially burned a smokeless grade of coke, but around 1869, a change was made to a grade of hard coal; later still a special type of anthracite was burned.

Specification:

Inside framed, side tank locomotive with two inclined outside cylinders 17¼in×24in, fitted with condensing apparatus.

Heating area: Tubes 903sq ft, firebox 90sq ft, total 993sq ft.

Grate area: 16sq ft.

Boiler pressure: 130/150lb/sq in.

Water capacity: 1,100gal.

Coal capacity: 1ton 7cwt.

Tractive effort: 12,850lb.

Brake type: Steam, later Westinghouse air system.

Livery:

Stock numbering:

Initially lettered 'A' to 'X' for first batch as booked by Beyer Peacock:

Year	MDR No	Works No
1871	1-24*	1063-1086
1876	25-30	1612-1617
1880	31-36	2053-2058
1883	37-42	2298-2303
1884	43-48	2584-2589
1886	49-54	2776-2781

* Later numbering.

Initially in a bright olive green with black lining and banding thinly edged with vermilion. Single panels on tank and bunker sides and also on cylinder cladding. Bright brass cleading between smokebox and boiler. Black chimney, smokebox, footplate and condenser pipes. Bright steel cylinder-end coves, pipe flanges and various levers and rods, including slide bars and coupling and connecting rods. Green wheels with black tyres and axle ends, the latter thinly edged in vermilion. Vermilion buffer sockets and face to buffer beams with black edging. Polished buffer heads and shanks. After 1886 a much darker green was adopted, without lining or banding. Tanks and bunker edged with a narrow black border. White lettering and numbers with black shading. Frames dark grey.

District Steam Stock from 1871

Under the 1866 agreement the District services were opened and worked by the MET, but District dissatisfaction was such that at the beginning of January 1870 notice was served on the MET, that the District would set up its own sheds and repair depots, order its own locomotives and stock and would commence its own workings on Monday 3 July 1871.

Drawing from the MET experience and looking for low-cost reliable carriages, a design was chosen similar to existing SECR and LCDR four-wheel stock, which was built on composite underframes, of perpendicular style, teak framed and panelled. Later batches had underframes of wrought-iron and, later still, of steel. Three body styles were built, namely four-compartment First Class, and five-compartment Second and Third Class, all with five-a-side seating. In brake vehicles of the latter two types, the brake end compartment was shared by the guard and passengers.

Later the passengers were moved out, and double doors were provided to ease the movement of luggage. All carriages had a plain arc roof style, and although reference has been made in the past to roof gas bags, similar to the MET town gas lighting system, many photographs circa 1875 show first order carriages having only large lamp tops on the roof and notes refer to 'near Pullman style oil lamps, with three shared between Second and Third Class carriages, and two only for First Class'. Pintsch lighting was introduced in 1878.

Altogether some 395 carriages of similar design were built between 1871 and 1900 — the first order originally in eight-car sets (which were also used in four-car sets). Later, all were regrouped into nine-car sets, and all orders subsequent to 1879 were for similar sets. Many Third Class and a few First Class carriages were transferred to Second Class operations, and one solitary First/Second Composite was adapted from a Second. The District assumed its independence on Tuesday 27 June 1871 and the first of the four-wheel stock took over District services on Monday, 3 July. These

Below:
A typical MDR four-wheel coach. If 20 is the original number then this may be one of the original Oldbury-built coaches of 1871. Many modifications have been carried out to the lighting and braking equipment. The vehicle is a Brake Third with a guard's position in the end compartment, as running in the late 1880s. *(U3310)*

Above right:
MDR four-wheel stock at the Mansion House. A familiar picture restored to something of its original tones. All trains were marked with destination boards front and rear, as well as smaller boards fitted when necessary at fascia board level, one to each coach. This stock has oil-gas lighting and is vacuum braked. The red tail lamp is built into the end bulkhead. *(22092)*

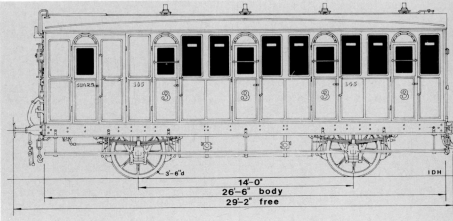

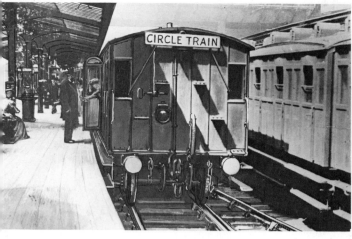

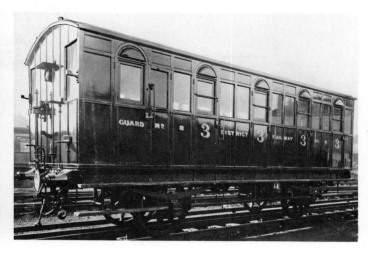

vehicles were very simply equipped with the Wilkins & Clark chain brake, but later the various versions of the Westinghouse brake were fitted in turn. Having started with four-wheel stock, the District continued with that form right to the end of steam days on Sunday 5 November 1905. Second Class accommodation was abolished with the withdrawal of the steam stock.

Above right:
MDR Brake Third No 8 as preserved circa 1920. The origin of this vehicle is not known, but it is fitted out with plain arc roof and oil-gas lighting. Vacuum brake fittings and screw couplings are also visible. Finished in varnished teak and hardwood, the lettering and numbering follows the former style of gilt, with white and blue dropped shadows. The vehicle has toplights, and double doors for the guard's compartment, and of which only the droplight in the latter is glazed. *(21389)*

Below left:
MDR Brake Third No 85 of 1879, and of either Ashbury or Met-Cam construction. Here the guard shared the end compartment with passengers, and had a wheel to apply the improved Webb chain brake. A Pintsch oil-gas cylinder below the floor feeds five staggered lamps, one per compartment. With partitions only shoulder high this gave an even light throughout the car. The teak finish is highly varnished, with plain gilt unshaded lettering. Each axlebox has the raised lettering 'MDR'. *LPC (0559)*

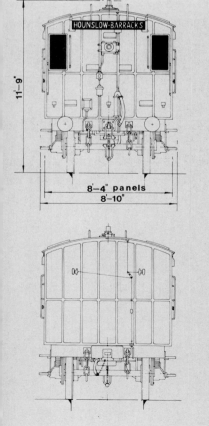

Specification:

1884 four-wheeled stock on steel underframes, with hardwood framed and panelled body. Provision for close coupling into semi-permanent sets. Standard screw couplings and buffing gear at outer ends. Pintsch high-pressure lighting. Later modifications to provide luggage space. Plain arc roof of canvas-covered boards. Full length double footboards. Westinghouse brake fitted.

Compartments: Four First, five Second or five Third (four on Brake Third). All with five-a-side seating. Sprung moquette upholstery in First Class with Rep seat squabs and backrests for Third Class. Less padded moquette for Second Class.

Marshalling: Formed generally into close-coupled sets as B3-3-2-1-1-2-3-3-B2.

Stock numbering:

The MDR appeared to commence its steam stock numbering in 1871 from unity for each class of car in the order First, Second and Third Class. Frequent conversions between new builds, took the next available numbers. The fifth new batch of stock took the following numbers:

Builder	Year	1	2(B*)	3(B*)
Ashbury	1884	71-82	92-109	141-164

* Some having a guard's compartment and brake gear, shared with passengers, later expanded into a combined guard/luggage space.

Four-wheel stock, both new and conversions, were constructed between the years 1871 and 1900. The final totals were 87 First Class (1-92); 92 Second Class (1-133); 215 Third Class (1-224); and one First/Second Class Composite (1), giving a grand total of 395 cars.

Livery:

Plain clear varnished teak. White lead on roof canvas. All underframe gear dark grey. Gilt numbering, blocked white and black. Wheels and tyres black. Light grey footboards.

Experimental Electric Stock 1899

The Metropolitan Railway took a cautious interest in electric traction as soon as it became a serious proposition after 1890. Many proposals were put to the company, nearly all later rejected. However, several schemes were introduced in the USA but like most new ideas there was no simple answer to electrification. But as the C&SLR had found, steering a course through Board of Trade restrictions left few possibilities and they chose one with somewhat restricted passenger capacity at that. It required having a motor coach at each end in which only the leading vehicle was powered whilst the train was operating. Having proved in 1898 that a

Below right:
A motor car of the Earl's Court electric experiments of 1899-1900. Basic design is similar to that of the Ashbury 'Bogie' stock. The raised frames at each end of the car provided plenty of clearance for the large 4ft diameter wheels. Inverted-channel section live rails were positioned 12.5in outside and 6in above the running rails. Apart from the whistle, nothing mars the roof line on any of the cars. *(H/6952)*

Top right:
One of two interesting reproductions appearing in an MDR brochure of 1899. Both were based on builders photographs and had been adapted by an artist to appear as coloured illustrations. Here they are shown cleaned up a little. The Third Class driving motor car was evidently not fitted out when the original photograph was taken as it is shown mounted on ordinary coach bogies, still with lower step boards fitted at axlebox level. The door to the passenger compartment is marked with a '3'. The only other lettering being 'Luggage Comp.' and 'Driver'. *(H/14668)*

Right:
The trailer car is a First/Third Composite with all compartments having the same basic dimensions, the only real difference being the better upholstered and equipped seating of the former class. A marked similarity to the body style of the MET 1899 steam-hauled 'Bogie' stock can be seen. The only markings on the coach appear to be an appropriate '1' or '3' on the doors. Both vehicles were identical in construction to the MET vehicles which formed part of the shared electric train experiment.
(H/14669)

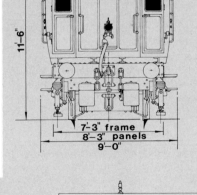

motor bogie could function (Wembley Park experiments) whilst fitted to one of the new bogie steam stock units (and for which three cars had been withdrawn), the MET were confident they could overcome the Board's resistance and be able to fill half the motor coach with passengers, and so increase the total passenger load.

In a joint undertaking with the MDR the MET agreed upon a six-coach train with two motor coaches running on a four-rail section of electrified track

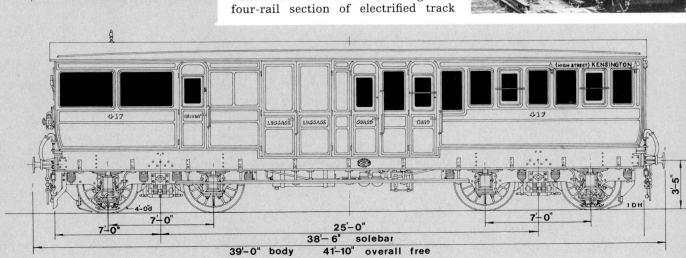

being used to prove the system. A new experimental train was therefore constructed by Brown, Marshalls on the lines of the 'Bogie' stock in which half the train was owned by each company.

The motor coaches were equipped with plain but functional plate-frame bogies with a gearless motor on each axle. Large 4ft spoked wheels were fitted to give plenty of clearance below, a feature which required raising the underframe at each end, and thus the floors thereon, well above platform level so making passenger access difficult. It was therefore necessary to have an open 'saloon' end to the motor-coach, which could be reached through a door at well level, the well already having to accommodate the guard and luggage compartment. Curious though the arrangement was, it could take passengers, though not with the same ease as the swing-door compartment layout of the trailer cars.

The train first ran on Saturday 9 December 1899 and then commenced a trial passenger service between Earl's Court and High Street Kensington on Monday 14 May 1900 until the set was withdrawn on Tuesday 6 November 1900. The operation appears to have been a success, for both companies commenced planning and circulating tenders for the overall electrification plan.

Specification:

Steel underframe, with steel and composition 'sandwich' flooring. Hardwood framed and panelled body. Plain arc roof of canvas-covered boards. Plate-frame double-equipped bogies with Siemens SA100hp traction motors. Siemens direct operating 'notch' contacts for series, series-parallel, and parallel control. Operation via a spoked handwheel. 'Notch' change by reference to an ammeter and voltmeter. Westinghouse air braking. Westinghouse compressor for brakes, sanding gear and whistle. Sprung shoes hung from axleboxes at leading and trailing positions, one side negative, the other positive. Busline connections in each car (though no control cables). Electric lighting.

Compartments: Seven Second or seven Third Class in Trailer Cars with five-a-side seating. Six in First Class vehicles, with five-a-side seating. Two First Class flanked each end by two Third Class in Composite vehicles with five-a-side seating. Both Second and Third Class Motor Cars seated 26.

Marshalling: 3M-3T-1/3T-1T-2T-2M.

Stock numbering:

Although numbers may have been allocated on paper, none were applied to the vehicles themselves during their period of service.

After subsequent conversion to standard trailer cars, ex-2nd trailer was numbered 415, 1st trailer 416 and motor car possibly 417. The latter at a much later date may have been converted to a service vehicle.

Livery:

Plain varnished teak body work, with white lead roof. The exposed sideframes above the top footboard painted in simulated teak. Bogie sideframes and underframe gear flat dark grey, with various polished fittings. References to the outer end buffer beams and sockets on motor coaches being vermilion have not been proven. Footboards in light grey. Fine gilt lettering for 'Driver', 'Guard', 'Luggage' and the respective classes, with white and blue blocking. No ownership markings were carried.

Metropolitan 'E' Class Locomotive
1897

The 0-4-4T design of 1897 by T. F. Clark was the first locomotive type wholly designed by the MET. Effectively it was an enlarged 'C' class having two 17¼in×26in inside cylinders and 5ft 6in driving wheels. Most were fitted with condensing apparatus and could work just as efficiently in tunnels as in the open. The first three were built at Neasden Works as Nos 77, 78 and 79 although the latter became No 1 when it entered service, taking the existing number of a withdrawn locomotive.

Orders for many more were planned, R. & W. Hawthorn Leslie & Co building Nos 79-82 from 1900-01, but possibly due to the advancement of electrification plans after that date, an intended order for a further seven locomotives of the class did not materialise.

The class worked to Aylesbury, and No 1 played a special part in the opening of the Uxbridge spur. Specially garlanded and bedecked with flags, flowers and white-painted coal, it left Baker Street at 11.07am on Monday, 4 July 1904. After a burst of speed through Neasden, a stop was made at Harrow to pick up the Uxbridge guests. Then at Rayners Lane Junction, the train was backed on to the Roxeth Viaduct. With a photographic stop at Ruislip, it then proceeded to Uxbridge for the celebration luncheon. There guests were able to examine one of the new electric train sets. No 1 and its train left Uxbridge at 3.50pm, stopping at Ruislip and Harrow, and reached Baker Street 40min later.

In spite of electrification, which only reached Rickmansworth, the locomotives maintained a fine service record, with four of the class being kept on as service stock (renumbered L44, L46, L47 and L48, lasting into the 1960s). L44 is preserved.

Left:

MET Class E 0-4-4T No 77 built at Neasden in 1896 to T. F. Clark's design, shown here in crimson lake livery lined out in three panels, the lining comprising a black band edged with straw. The dome is of polished brass. The original MET heraldic design is placed on the sandbox. The bright brass smokebox/boiler beading and splasher segment can be seen. *Bucknall Collection/Ian Allan Library*

Above:

A smart MET 'main line' steam train at Neasden c1905. Class E 0-4-4T No 77 was the first of the class built at Neasden and is ready to haul a six-car set of Ashbury 'Bogie' stock, with an older four-wheel 'Jubilee' brake van bringing up the rear. The leading car is a Brake Second No 375 built in 1898. All vehicles except the brake van are in a varnished teak finish with white fascia and waist panels. *(49952)*

Specification:

Inside frames, with two 17¼in×26in inside cylinders. Slide valves with Stevenson valve gear. Fitted with condensing apparatus.

Heating area: Tubes 1,050sq ft, firebox 95.6sq ft, total 1,145.6sq ft.

Grate area: 16.7sq ft.

Boiler pressure: 160lb/sq in.

Tractive effort: 15,420lb.

Water capacity: 1,250gal.

Coal capacity: 2ton 4cwt.

Stock numbering:

Year	Neasden		Hawthorn Leslie	
	MET No		Met No	Works No
1896	77-78		—	—
1898	(79) changed to 1		—	—
1900/01	—		79-82	2474-77

Livery:

Boiler cladding, tanks, cab, bunker, splasher (with bright brass trim), footplate valance and wheels crimson lake. Black smokebox, chimney (with brass numbers) and condenser pipes. Vermilion buffer beams. Polished steel coupling rods, handrails, smokebox door hinges and fittings. Polished brass surrounds to cab spectacle plates. Tank and bunker panelled out. Black lining thinly edged with gilt. Boiler banding similar. Black footplate. Various other bright steel, copper and brass fittings. Inner edge of tyre and axle ends relieved with gilt lining. Lined-out footplate valance and footsteps. Dark grey frames.

Metropolitan 'Bogie' Stock 1898

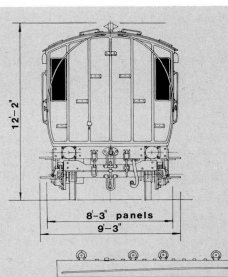

With bogied stock coming into use on several main line railways, the MET, with a mind to its surface Extension services, examined the possibilities of introducing an experimental train of bogie stock c1890. The earlier 'Jubilee' four-wheel stock had shown an overall improvement in comfort and running characteristics, but considerable scope for further progress remained. The Board were looking for an extended 'Jubilee' body on a steel underframe to the same 38ft 10in overall length as the eight-wheel rigid stock, the new speci-

Below:
Steam 'Bogie' stock for the MET Extension Lines brought a more comfortable standard of accommodation for country travellers. Brake Third No 381 and Third Class coach No 377 sport the more usual tumblehome of contemporary railway stock. Note also the close coupling of the coaches. *Ian Allan Library*

Above right:
Preserved driving trailer car No 400 was originally a standard 'Bogie' stock Second Class coach built in 1900 by Met-Cam. Here it shows well the later MET livery of varnished teak, with chrome yellow lining, gilt lettering and numbering with dropped blue shading. *(LTE 26)*

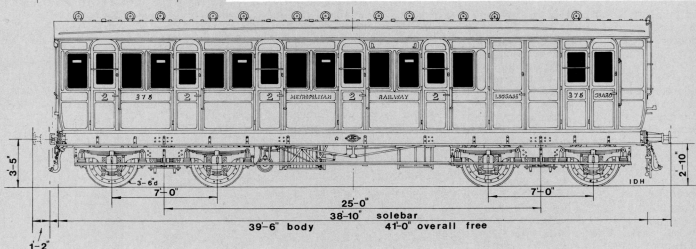

fication to include steam heating, electric lighting, automatic vacuum braking, bogies with two cast iron brake shoes per wheel, simplified glazing, arch roof and roof mounted ventilation. Such stock would be capable of operation both in the tunnel sections and out on the surface 'main line' with equal comfort.

The fulfilment of this specification resulted in considerable delay, and at the end of 1896 it was decided to rearrange the original layouts and prepare new drawings for three classes of carriage, all with a five-a-side seating. First Class vehicles featured six compartments while those of Second and Third Class contained seven. Brake vehicles with guard and luggage space had five compartments. Multi-layer floors were introduced with felt sandwiched between metal and wood for sound insulation. A production order for four six-coach trains was placed with Ashbury — the stock entering service during the early part of 1898.

Successful service performance resulted in further orders placed with several builders, and three of the first batch of cars had hardly entered traffic before being converted for electrification experiments at Wembley Park. The arrival of the 'Bogie' stock also saw the introduction of 'flattened' door tops in which the original fully radiused top edge was replaced by smaller radiused corners joined by a short straight edge.

Specification:

Steel underframe, hardwood framed and panelled body. Plain arc roof of canvas-covered boards, with Laycock torpedo ventilation. Laycock steam heating, Stones electric lighting and automatic vacuum brake. Fox 7ft pressed steel bogies with Mansell disc wheels. 'Flat' topped doors. Sound deadened floors. Single full length footboards level with bottom edge of solebar.

Compartments: Six in First Class vehicles, seven in both Second and Third Class. Brake Seconds and Brake Thirds both contained five compartments, while Composite stock featured three Firsts and three Thirds. Some First Class accommodation initially offered four-a-side seating; later all classes were standardised at five-a-side. Moquette upholstery of differing qualities was provided throughout, as were sprung roller blinds.

Marshalling: B2-2-1-1/3-3-B3.

Stock numbering:

Ledger numbering relative to class:

Builder	Year	B2	2	1	1/3	3	B3
Ashbury	1898	373	369	361	365	377	381
Ashbury	1898	374	370	362	366	378	382
Ashbury	1898	375	371	363	367	379	383
Ashbury	1898	376	372	364	368	380	384
Met-Cam	1900	395	400	405	410	390	385
Cravens	1900	396	401	406	411	391	386
Cravens	1900	397	402	407	412	392	387
Ashbury	1900	398	403	408	413	393	388
Ashbury	1900	399	404	409	414	394	389

Livery:

Natural clear varnished teak, lined out in straw. Gilt lettering and numbering blocked with white and blue shading. Roof canvas white lead. Solebars painted to simulate teak. Light grey footboards. Bogie frames and most other underframe gear dark grey. Wheels dark indian red (later black), tyres white.

District 'A' Stock 1903

The MDR went ahead with electrification much more rapidly than the MET, placing orders with Brush in 1900 for two seven-car trains, one fitted with BWE equipment, the other with BT-H, for comparative trials on the Ealing and South Harrow line.

The cars were largely of wooden construction on 48ft underframes, and followed very closely the layout of electric rolling stock already in use in the USA where more or less identical cast-steel motor and trailer bogie designs were used.

Motor cars were equipped with a single power bogie with a traction motor driving each axle, having a trailer bogie at the opposite end. In this respect the MDR vehicles differed from those on the MET, each of which featured two bogies and four traction motors.

Other features of the MDR stock — namely centre couplers and plain buffing plates, Monitor roof section, compressed air brake and with multiple unit control — were closely allied to US practice. Leading motor cars had a generous luggage compartment: the passenger areas on all cars were of the open saloon type, with double sliding centre doors and gate ends. The vehicles seemed bright, spacious and quite unique when they first appeared in March 1903. Unusual also were the centre motor cars which had boxed controls at either end platform so that a train could be split into a smaller formation if required; these centre cars could be driven as single units if necessary. Later a couple of trailers had controls fitted at one end, so that a split train could operate as two separate units.

Actual operations commenced on Tuesday 23 June 1903 as far as Park Royal — a full service to South Harrow commencing five days later. Generally the two trains performed well, though the BT-H traction equipment and Sprague-BT-H control was more reliable than similar Westinghouse equipments, although the Westinghouse air brake was found to be superior to the Christensen form fitted to the BT-H train.

Top:
One of the four-car sets from the two MDR experimental 'A' stock trains of 1903 seen at South Harrow on the 'down' line. This may be formed (l to r) of Nos 4, 301, 202 and 3, and could well be in the gamboge and lake livery. Fuses are only mounted above the trailer shoebeams on this side. All beams appear to carry them on the opposite side.
Ian Allan Library

Above:
MDR 1903 Third Class trailer No 308 converted with a half-cab to a control trailer. Although the arched window style remains, the lower side panelling has been replaced with a form similar to the later 'B' stock cars. As well as the half gate at the driving end, the full gate ends remain on this and the rest of the stock. Collector beams are mounted on the standard trailer bogie. *(U3358)*

Top right:
MDR 'A' electric stock barely visible behind the newly built car shed at the South Harrow terminus in 1903. This view, looking east, was taken from a public footbridge, which separated the sheds and storage tracks from the signalbox and station buildings, 100yd or so to the west. The stock had not been in the open air long enough to get the white lead roof boards dirtied when the photograph was taken. *LPC (3350)*

Following the trials, selected items of approved equipments were written into a tender specification for an order for production electric stock. In service the two trial trains remained on MDR branch lines, being used for crew and other staff training in addition to their revenue-earning duties. Some structural modifications were carried out on the driving ends of motor cars at a later date to enable the use of headcode lamps and destination boards.

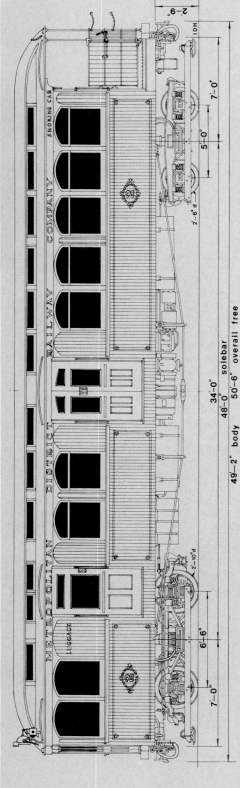

Specification:

Composite underframe on motor cars, hardwood underframe on trailer cars. Hardwood framed and panelled body with Monitor roof section. Cast steel bogies. Open gate ends. First train: Sprague, Thompson-Houston non-automatic nine-notch electro-magnetic control with GE66 traction motors. Christensen air brake. Second train: Westinghouse automatic electro-pneumatic 'turret' control, with 83M traction motors. Westinghouse brake.

Both trains offered Third Class open accommodation only with plain rattan seating, running longitudinally on end and centre motor cars, seating 38 and 48 respectively. Trailer cars with mixed longitudinal and transverse seating could accommodate 52 seated passengers.

Marshalling: 3M(E)-3T-3T-3M(M)-3T-3T-3M(E)
later as
3M(E)-3T-3T-3M(M)+3CT-3T-3M(E).

Stock numbering:

Builder	Year	Type	Initial numbering	1910 renumbering
Brush	1903	3M(E)	1- 4	1- 4
Brush	1903	3M(M)	201-202	130-131
Brush	1903	3T	301-308	301-308*

* With two later conversions to Control Trailer cars.

Livery:

Details of experimental liveries applied to 'A' stock vehicles are uncertain. Initially it would seem that an American 'Interurban Gamboge' (yellow) body colour was applied, panelled and lined out in dark crimson lake, the areas of application including the waist rail and lower portion of the door frames, a narrow border along the base of the side and end panels and the area below the door sills. Lettering and numbering was in gilt with blocked shading. The driving window was in a light oak frame (possibly a counter-balanced sash type) with a clear lacquer finish somewhat lighter in hue than the gamboge, and could be released and lowered partially to give the driver a clear view ahead in an emergency.

Roof canvas was white lead, whilst underframe equipment and bogie frames were dark grey with various polished areas. The motor car shoebeam cradle was originally black, although on the trailer cars they were light grey. Later the shortened versions were light grey.

Several experimental schemes were tried which included Pullman olive green, with gilt lining and also bright scarlet with gilt and black lining. The latter was said to have been 'glaring' and did not wear well. A dark scarlet was later tried.

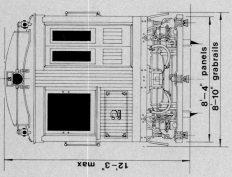

Metropolitan Electric Stock 1905

The Metropolitan Railway took a slower approach to electrification than its companion, the District company. Initially it was intended to run electric traction only from Baker Street to Uxbridge. This decision having been made there was considerable uncertainty as to the size and layout for its proposed stock and the selection of suitable electrical equipment for installation thereon.

The first proposal made in late 1899 was for a lengthened version of 'Bogie' compartment stock. Draft layouts showed a nine-compartment Third Class Trailer car and a seven-compartment Motor Car, the latter having a driving and luggage compartment approximately 11ft in length, both vehicles featuring a 51ft 6in body with all electrical equipment beneath the car floor. However, it is likely that study of the (then) latest US electric railway technology and the newly opened Central London Railway caused the Metropolitan management to think again.

Second proposals dated 1900 discussed layouts which presented a 'CLR-type Trailer Car', with its solebar underside raised some 3ft above rail level, and the body lengthened to 51ft 6in. These resulted in a car with a Monitor roof, 4ft end platforms guarded by metal swing gates, and some 16 sets of small fanlighted windows along each body side. The increase in size raised seating capacity from 48 to 56. The Motor Car layout was similar to the rear of the 11ft driver and luggage compartment, the latter having a 3ft sliding door.

Two Fox pressed steel bogies each carried two nose-suspended traction motors. Orders for trailer cars of this

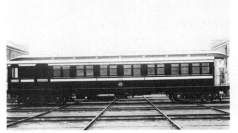

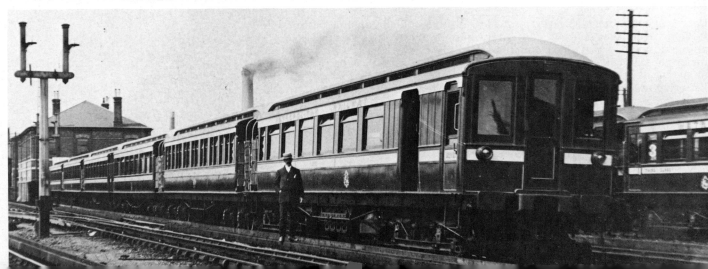

type were placed with Brown, Marshalls in 1902, and with the selection of Westinghouse equipment many months later an order for matching motor cars was placed with Metropolitan-Cammell Ltd. Later the need to operate three-car sets on the Uxbridge line saw the introduction of cabbed Trailer Firsts equipped with controls as driving trailers.

The combination of early trials and later thinking, produced some all round revisions to the original layouts, which were incorporated in a subsequent order for more stock. The Uxbridge service started in part on Monday 1 January 1905, but it was some three months before the full service was all-electric. Some of the stock was delivered with enclosed vestibule ends to test passenger reaction and improve weather protection. The response indicated that the latter was considered essential.

Far left:
MET 1904 motor car No 3 is seen here in the original varnished teak and white finish. All lower side panelling was of metal sheet and was painted to simulate teak. Bright polished axlebox covers and gates are clearly visible, as are grey bogie frames, black wheels and white tyres. Note that the sidelights are grouped in pairs. Original light pressed-steel bogies. *Ian Allan Library*

Below left:
Original MET 1904 motor car No 9 in later life with enclosed vestibule and double centre doors fitted. Shown in an all-teak finish and with the heavier pressed-steel bogies. The full depth driving lights were retained. Years of grime have conditioned the white roof to a dingy grey. *Ian Allan Library*

Centre left:
One of the first batch of 1905 BWE 150 stock motor cars, No 14, is seen here experimentally fitted with an extra door at the forward end of the passenger saloon. The car has already had its open end fully vestibuled and has had double sliding doors added after 1911. *(U14031)*

Bottom:
A six-car multiple-unit train of MET 1904 BWE 150 stock. The driving motor car, and the third and fourth vehicles have the later batch double-size windows, as opposed to the smaller paired windows of the original stock. The early form of current collection by means of shoes mounted at the extreme ends of the channel section carriers attached to the axleboxes, is still being used. *(H/17174)*

Specification:

Steel underframes, hardwood frames and upper panelwork, with brass and steel sheet lower panelling. Monitor section roof and open gate-ended platforms. Steel and Induroleum flooring. Motor cars double-equipped, with pressed steel bogies and BWE 50M 150hp traction motors, with spur gearing ratio 17 : 54. Westinghouse electro-pneumatic 'turret' control. Westinghouse 8G2 compressor and automatic brake. Standard screw couplings at outer ends of sets, otherwise centre link and pin coupling (later buckeye auto-coupler). Full length single footboard.

Layout: Open saloon interiors — First Class seating 56, Third Class 56 and Third Class Motor Coaches 48. First Class seats covered with plush moquette, Third Class with Buffalo hide, all fitted with electric under-seat heating.

Marshalling: 3M-3T-1T-1T-3T-3M, (although seven-car sets were intended, they were too long for platforms). Later the following formation was used: 3M-3T-1DT+1DT-3T+3M.

Stock numbering:

Builder	Year	3M	1T*	3T
Met-Cam	1904	1-20	1-20	1-30
Met-Cam	1904	21-56	21-56	31-56

* These cars were later converted to Driving Trailers.

Livery:

Natural clear varnished teak, with lower metal panels painted, grained and stippled to simulate the teak finish with white fascia and waist panels. Roof canvas white lead. End gates and supports, bright steel alloy finish. Solebars, bogie side frames and most underframe gear dark grey. Gilt lettering and numbering, blocked white and blue. One full colour heraldic crest per side. Light grey footboards. Original shoebeam cradle black, with bright steel shoes and attachments. Wheels black, tyres white.

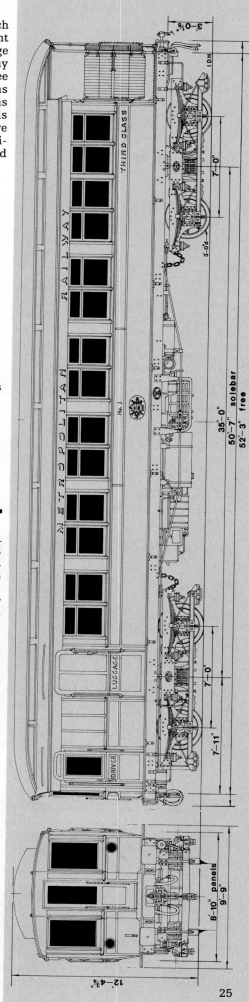

Metropolitan Electric Stock 1906

Ordered in 1904, a second batch of cars from Metropolitan-Cammell had a simplified window layout, in which each closely set pair was replaced with a large single window having two opening fanlights. Other small modifications were included, otherwise the same type of Westinghouse equipments were fitted. Large roller-blind destination boxes were placed over the driving cabs. As before, the cars were largely constructed of teak and mahogany, but the lower side panels and the floors were sheet metal, the latter being overlaid with a thick fire-resistant Induroleum composition. The interiors were finished in natural oak. The original motor bogies were of light construction with elliptical bolster springs, and these were later replaced with a similar but heavier bogie having coil bolster springing. All motor bogies carried the revised shoebeam.

By 1906 the open platform ends were found to be most undesirable for surface working and a start was made on the provision of all cars with end vestibules. The original stock was coupled together in sets by a simple link and pin projecting through a short, sprung central buffer. The outer ends had provision for similar fittings, but were also fitted with two further buffing plates set at the standard distance apart and screw couplings, so that in an emergency the sets could be coupled to a steam locomotive or steam stock if required.

Later an American-style buckeye automatic centre coupler replaced the link and pin system, and with a view to reducing stopping times at stations additional centre doorways, similar to those of MDR stock, were fitted, necessitating a rearrangement of the seating layout. Although contemplated as early as 1909, the first conversions did not take place until 1911.

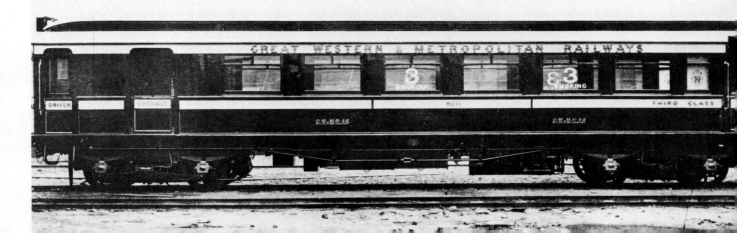

Below left:
A 1906 BWE 200 stock motor car, No 70, seen in original form but with the double-door conversion. *(23797)*

Bottom left:
H & C 1906 motor car No 11 in the original varnished teak and white finish. The larger single sidelights of late 1905 and 1906 identify it as being of the later stock. Axlebox covers are polished while the rest of the bogie area is grey. Wheels are black. The vestibule door slides into a pocket in which the last small sidelight has opal glass with a darker motif emblazoned. *(16894)*

Below:
A 1906 Third Class trailer in original form but with door conversions, No 61 was in the last batch of original MET electric stock built. With the question of door size and position being a matter for strong debate by 1912, the issue was not then resolved and extra stock then ordered was almost identical to the 1906 style, save for the use of an elliptical roof section. *(U14017)*

Specification:

Steel underframes, hardwood frames and upper panel work, with lower panelling of brass and steel sheet. Monitor section roof and open gate-ended platforms. Motor cars double-equipped, with pressed steel bogies and BWE 50M 150hp traction motors with spur gearing ratio 17 : 54. Westinghouse electro-pneumatic 'turret' control. Westinghouse 8G2 compressor and automatic brake. Standard screw couplings fitted at the outer ends of sets, or alternatively the centre link and pin variety. Later, the stock was fitted with buckeye automatic couplers. Full length single footboard.

Layout: Open saloon interiors — First Class seating 56, Third Class 56 and Third Class Motor Coaches 48. First Class seats covered with plush moquette, Third Class with Buffalo hide, all fitted with electric under-seat heating.

Marshalling: 3M-3T-1DT+
    1DT-3T-3M.

Stock numbering:

Following on from first order:

Builder	Year	3M	1DT	3T
Met-Car	1905-06	57-70	57-76	57-76
Met-Car	1906	71-82	—	

Livery:

Natural clear varnished teak, with lower metal panels painted, grained and stippled to simulate the teak finish, with white fascia and waist panels. Roof canvas white lead. End gates and supports, bright steel alloy finish. Solebars, bogie side frames and most underframe equipment dark grey. Gilt lettering and numbering, blocked white and blue. Wheels black, tyres white. Two full-colour heraldic crests per side. Light grey footboards and shoebeams. Blind box with 5in lettering, white on black.

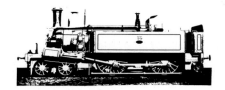

Metropolitan Electric Locomotive 1906 (BWE)

At the turn of the century, the Metropolitan Railway required a number of electric locomotives capable of hauling heavy passenger trains originating from country areas over the electrified section to Baker Street. It therefore considered an American Bo-Bo 'camel back' design following the style of the CLR electric locomotives of 1900. Ten locomotives were ordered eventually, with bodies by Metropolitan-Cammell and Westinghouse control and traction equipment.

The thinking behind the body design was that one set of centrally placed controls would suffice for travel in either direction. In practice, the driver was isolated in a rather unnatural

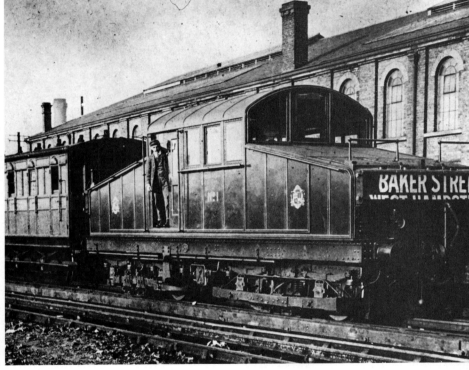

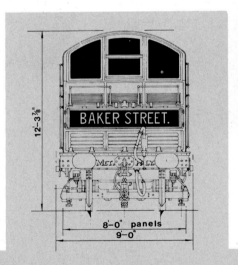

Above:
BWE 1904 electric locomotive No 1 in MET livery is seen here coupled to a train of eight-wheel rigid stock. The effectiveness of these locomotives was diminished to some extent by electrical problems; also the single centrally-placed controller limited the driver's visibility ahead. Later two control units were provided. Problems with the shoegear were only overcome after experimentation with several forms of beam attachment. *(H/10678)*

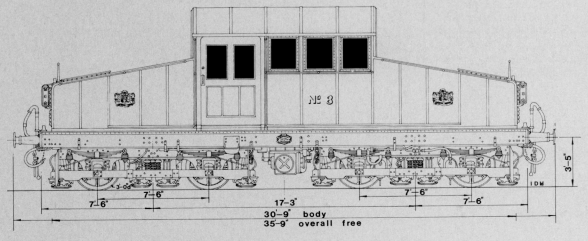

Below:

In this photograph, BWE 'camelback' electric locomotive No 1 is hauling a six-car set of Ashbury 'Bogie' stock; the leading car is Brake Third No 383 built in 1898. While this vacuum braked set could be hauled equally well by steam or electric traction, no current pick-up facility was provided for the latter mode of operation. The locomotive is lined out in crimson lake; the cars are in varnished teak, with white fascia and waist panels. Note the express headlamp code. *(754644)*

Left:

Twin headlamps and the 'Baker Street' destination would suggest that No 1 is about to take over a London-bound train at Harrow. *LPC (1784)*

location with very poor visibility, and the locomotives were instantly disliked. A large sliding door was provided on each side.

Pressed steel bogies were fitted, reinforced with much extra platework, and carried very long shoebeams with shoes mounted at the extremities, well beyond the bogie end frames. Large, electrically-illuminated roller-blind destination boxes were placed at each body end. Equipment for dual braking was fitted, together with standard screw couplings and buffers. Sanding gear was also carried. Brake rigging of the inside type was heavy with one shoe per wheel, and both systems could be operated simultaneously.

In operation the locomotives were reasonably successful, at least on the MET surface main line. Over the tunnel sections trouble was experienced with the shoes fouling the District live rail, and drivers experienced an almost total lack of visibility over the locomotive ends. Efforts were made to alter the

lamp iron and destination box assembly and dual sets of controls, each located forward and to the side of the cab in either direction, replaced the single unit. Revised shoe beam gear

was also fitted. Although the modifications effected a general improvement, at the same time the poor reliability of the Westinghouse equipment became manifest.

Specification:

Steel underframe, with steel framed and panelled main body. Steel framed hardwood doors. Wooden window framing. Light pressed steel bogies with four BWE type 86M, 200hp traction motors (boosted to 250hp by extra ventilation), with spur gearing ration 22 : 60. BWE electro-pneumatic 'turret' control. Twelve-shoe current pick-up. Westinghouse 862 compressor. Two Gresham & Craven exhausters. Power sanding.

Tractive effort: 20,600lb approx.

Brake type: Dual fitted for Westinghouse and vacuum operation.

Stock numbering:

Builder	Year	MET Nos
Met-Cam	1906	1-10

Livery:

Crimson lake body with black mouldings edged in straw. White lead roof sheets. Solebars crimson lake. Numbered in 5in gilt characters blocked red and black. Vermilion buffer beams marked 'Met Ry' in gilt blocked black. Buffer sockets black, with polished steel buffer faces and shanks. All underframe equipment flat dark grey. Two heraldic crests per side; 12in destination blind letters, white on black. Original steel shoe gear cradle black. Handrails, collector shoes and attachment blocks polished steel.

District 'B' Stock 1905

The initial 'A' stock had been most successful, and the District therefore placed an order for 60 seven-car trains of an improved type, to cover the entire electrification programme. The order was so big that sub-contracting on a large scale was necessary, and so as to obtain the complete orders by 1905 much of the work went to continental builders.

The 'A' stock basic design was retained but the detail was much improved. Enclosed end vestibules with single sliding side doors, and single end

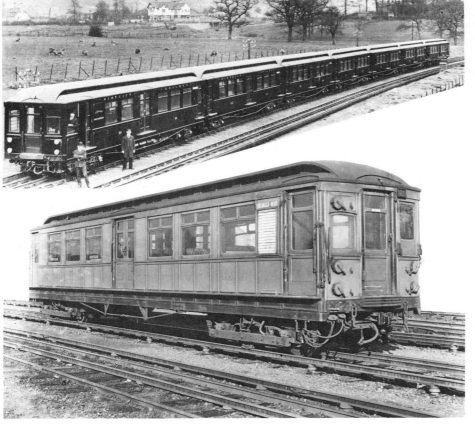

centre doors, gave better weather proofing. The basic trailer body on a wooden underframe had three large side lights either side of the pair of centre sliding doors, each with a pair of inward opening fan lights. The MDR had a need to maintain a number of First Class Trailer Cars for certain services, but appeared to make no differentiation between Third and First Class in the order book, although at least one trailer car in five was equipped for First Class use, according to footnotes.

There were three types of motor car all mounted on steel underframes — end motor cars with and without a luggage compartment, and centre motor cars with an enclosed driving compartment at each end. Initially all side doors on each car were air operated by the 'gateman'. However, it soon became so unreliable that the equipment was removed and hand operation was again resorted to. Control of the traction motors was by the low-voltage Sprague Thompson Houston multiple units system which required a bus line throughout the train. Current collection was necessary only on the motor car bogies.

This stock had a surprisingly long service life. Later the luggage compartments were removed, thus extending the seating in end motor cars. Problems with the original American pattern cast steel bogies led to several changes. Heavier plate framed 'A2' motor bogies were introduced and trials were undertaken with at least two types of intermediate trailer bogie.

Top left:
A seven-car set of MDR 'B' stock photographed early in 1905 on the up line just west of Sudbury Hill station. In the background, a few hundred yards away, work is in progress on the construction of the GCR station. This train is thought to have the original crimson lake and gilt paint scheme, with the nearest three cars being Nos 10, 332 and 326. *(H/12852)*

Centre:
MDR 'B' stock motor car No 349 of 1905. This was originally a Met-Car built trailer car which had undergone conversion to run mixed stock trains of 'C', 'D' and 'E' stock. The vehicle is shown in later life and has an overhaul date of Februry 1924 marked upon it. *(U3360)*

Bottom:
MDR 'B' Stock motor car No 30 is seen in this photograph taken around 1905 at the time of a press review. Reported to be painted a 'deep scarlet with gold lettering and lining' by a Topical Press team, this looks like the crimson lake livery. All doors and window frames show a less glossy lacquered appearance. *(U11970)*

Specification:

Steel underframed motor cars; composite underframe with hardwood frames and panelling for trailer cars. Monitor roof section. Motor cars single equipped on US designed cast steel Type 'A' bogies with BT-H GE69 200hp traction motors. 'B' cast steel equalised beam type trailer bogies. All cars originally fitted with pneumatic door operation, later replaced by hand operation. BT-H electro-magnetic control. All motor cars fitted with compressors. Westinghouse brake. All stock subject to bogie replacement.

Layout: Semi-open saloon form seating 40 in Third Class motor cars with luggage compartment and 48 in those without; Third Class centre motor cars seated 48; First and Third Class trailers seated 48 with the additional option of making four occasional seats available. Rattan seating.

Marshalling: Generally, 3M(E)-3T-1T-3M(M)+3M(M)-3T-3M(E), for seven car sets. However, the need to provide First Class accommodation only on certain routes complicated the make-up. Four-car sets were also required, so that with six-, seven-, eight- and nine-car sets being needed at different times, the variations were great. As far as possible each set had an equal number of motor cars and trailers.

Stock numbering:

Because of so much sub-contract working, an effort appears to have been made to space out the numbering in columns of five. Having started thus, the enumerator changed halfway through the order, to another form. Numbers followed 'A' stock.

Builder	Car Type	MDR Numbering
Brush	End Motor	Numbered in 5s, 5 to 100
Met-Cam	End Motor	6-9, 11-14, 16-19, 21-24, 26-29,
Ateliers (France)		
(Luneville)	End Motor	31-34, 36-39, 41-44, 46-49, 51-54,
(Blanc Misseron)	End Motor	56-59, 61-64, 66-69, 71-74, 76-79, 81-84, 86-89, 91-94, 96-99, 101-104, 106-109, 111-114, 116-119, 121-124, 126-129
Brush	Middle Motor	203-214
Met-Cam	Middle Motor	215-220, 222-226, 264
Ateliers (Luneville)	Middle Motor	221, 227-263, 265-274
Brush	Trailer	309-346
Met-Cam	Trailer	347-384
Ateliers (Pantin)	Trailer	385-404, 470-480, 526-536
Ateliers (Ivry)	Trailer	405-425, 481-501
Ateliers (St Denis)	Trailer	426-469, 502-525

Livery:

Crimson lake (deep scarlet) body, with stained and lacquered doors and window frames to a near matching hue. White lead roof sheets. Gilt lining and lettering blocked white and blue. Bogie frames and underframe equipment dark grey. Black wheels and tyres light grey. Several livery changes followed at intervals.

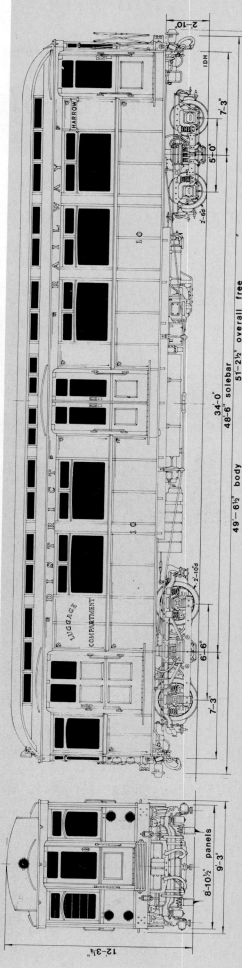

District Electric Locomotive 1905

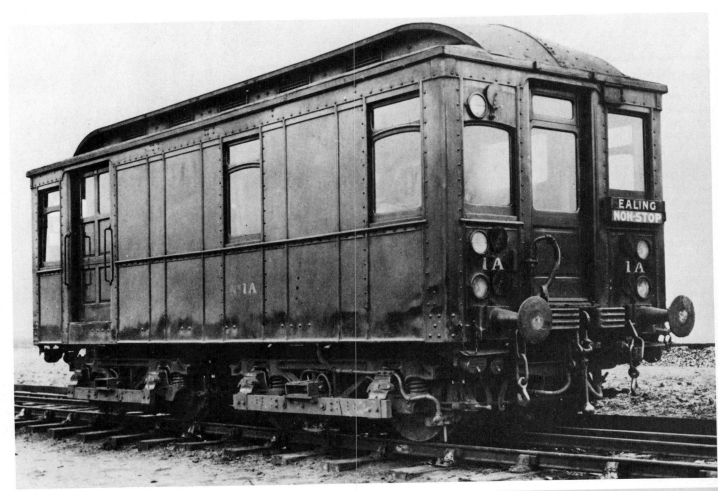

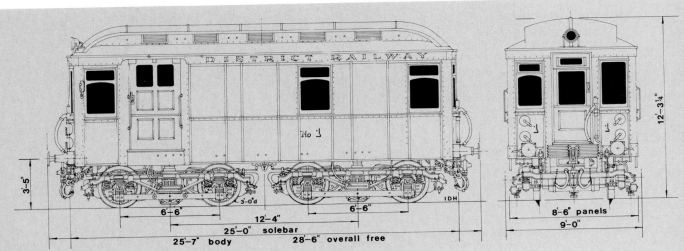

Electrification of sections of the MET and entire MDR systems led to great improvements in the atmosphere for travellers. However, working arrangements with LNWR and GWR trains running over parts of the system still caused some pollution as they were steam-hauled. The MDR therefore arranged for the LNWR trains to be worked by some new electric locomotives, between Earl's Court and Mansion House.

Ten of these locomotives were constructed by Met-Cam, and each were fitted out with four GE69 traction motors, mounted in a pair of the standard cast steel 'A' type bogies. Some thought was applied beforehand, and for ease of working on tight curves it was decided to build the locomotives as compact short-wheelbase units, which could work in pairs for normal steam stock operations, as such trains were considerably heavier than the contemporary electric stock. Trials during November 1905 with both single and paired units of the all-steel design proved most successful, and the MDR took over the LNWR workings on Monday 4 December. The new locomotives had the driving ends and general styling of the MDR 'B' electric stock and with just enough clearance for the two motor bogies not to foul each other, the body length was 25ft 7in.

After some three years of operation, the MDR expansion of services on the surface lines to the west of Hammersmith required the cutting back of 'foreign' trains using MDR tracks as on the Outer Circle service of the LNWR. Thus, as of New Year's Day 1909 the LNWR service was terminated at Earl's Court and the electric locomotives became temporarily redundant. Meanwhile, negotiations had started between the LTSR and GWR for some further through train services. The former commencing a through Southend service on Wednesday 1 June 1910, where again paired MDR electric locomotives hauled the trains between Ealing Broadway and Barking. The GWR eventually used electric locomotives supplied by the MET.

Three locomotives were scrapped a year later and from 1922 the remainder were overhauled and fitted out with GE260 type traction equipments removed from MDR 'F' stock. The LTSR service was finally terminated at the end of September 1939 as a wartime economy.

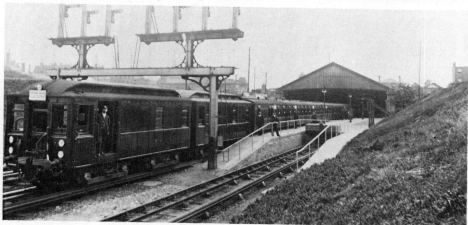

Left:
The MDR 'Box-cab' locomotive No 1A, a 1905 design, had many similarities with the 'B' Stock—in particular with the style of the driving ends.
 The fitting of side buffers was necessary as the task of the paired locomotives was the hauling of steam stock over the underground lines. In later life, after modifications, at least two became service locomotives at District Line depots. *(22018)*

Top:
MDR locomotives Nos 2a and 8a coupled in multiple for 'steam' stock haulage. LT sources state that, with revised couplings at one end, a pair could be set at either end of a set of four electric cars and operated as a multiple unit train on some services. In the same form, the locomotives went on yard duties with a suitably equipped match truck coupled at whichever end was appropriate. *(23381)*

Above:
MDR locomotives Nos 7 and 7a about to haul a 'Through Train — Ealing & Southend' (as the headboard reads) from the District platforms at Ealing Broadway, on behalf of the LTSR around June 1910. The latter company produced special stock for this service, the vehicles being described as having a 'varnished teak' livery. Each bore a similar board to that mounted on the leading locomotive. *(H7973)*

Specification:

All steel underframed and bodied locomotive. Hardwood panelled doors and window frames. Double-equipped with cast steel Type 'A' motor bogies, and four GE69 traction motors. BT-H electro-magnetic control.
 Later fitted with plate frame, double-equipped motor bogies from 1920 'F' stock motor cars. These Type 'E' bogies carrying two GE260 traction motors with tapped field system.

Tractive effort: 10,000lb approximately.
Brake type: Westinghouse.

Stock numbering:

The numbering was to suit paired operation:

Builder	Year	MDR numbering
Met-Cam	1905	1-1A, 2-2A, 3-3A, 4-4A, 5-5A

Livery:

Originally crimson lake (deep scarlet) body, with stained and lacquered doors and window frames to a near matching hue. White lead roof sheets. Gilt lining and lettering, blocked white and blue. Bogie frames and underframe equipment dark grey. Black wheels and tyres. Light grey shoebeam. Several livery changes followed.

Metropolitan Electric Locomotive 1907 (BT-H)

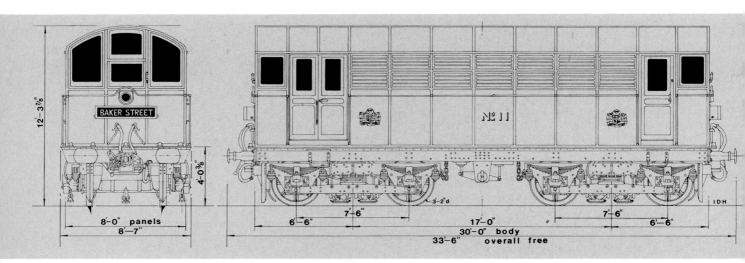

BAKER STREET

12'-3⅜"
4'-0⅜"
8'-0" panels
8'-7"
6'-6"
7'-6"
3'-2"d
N⁰ 11
17'-0"
30'-0" body
33'-6" overall free
7'-6"
6'-6"
1DH

Below:
MET 'Box cab' electric locomotive No 11 of 1907 passes Willesden Green Junction signalbox. Fitted out with BT-H control and traction equipments, they were an improvement over the BWE locomotives. However, they were still not the final solution to electric locomotive requirements as operations were soon to prove.
LPC(2734)

By June 1906, an order for 10 locomotives was placed by the MET with BT-H. The new locomotives had driving positions at each extremity of a square ended 'box cab' body, and carried BT-H control and traction equipments, the latter motors being installed in similar but slightly heavier pressed steel bogies. Shoebeam gear followed that already established for the later batches of BWE electric stock whereby the shorter oak beam was attached to lugs on each axlebox and carried two positive shoes halfway along each beam. Negative shoes were suspended directly from each motor casing

Dual braking and sanding gear was fitted. These locomotives also saw the inclusion of buckeye centre coupler pockets fitted below the otherwise standard screw-coupling. The actual couplers could be fitted for emergency use in propelling stalled electric stock.

Illuminated destination blind boxes were initially fitted to the cab ends, but these were replaced around 1912 by the more standard enamelled iron headboards. Electric headlights were also provided in addition to oil lamp irons. In general the new BT-H locomotives were a great improvement over the BWE types.

The box body gave better ventilation and improved access to any internal equipment, the latter aided by the provision of large inward-opening double doors on each side, in addition to the driver's door. Three vertical windows were provided at each end, the centre ones having adjustable portions. The doors to the driving compartments were fitted with droplights.

The first of the locomotives entered service in September 1907, and all the others had followed by the end of that year. When ordering new electric coaching stock in 1912 the MET had to consider a complete rebalance of the stock of traction equipment sets between BWE and BT-H-equipped electric saloon stock. The opportunity was taken on that occasion to exchange the 10 sets of BT-H locomotive equipment with new BWE equipment so that all 20 locomotives had similar equipment even though the bogies were of a longer wheelbase with heavier plate frame construction. Finally, a total rebuild of all electric locomotives was planned in 1919, though only two were in fact adapted. After a look at costings it was decided to go for completely new constructions.

Specification:

Steel underframe with steel-framed and panelled main body. Steel-framed hardwood doors. Wood window framing. Initially light pressed steel bogies with four BT-H GE69 200hp nose-suspended traction motors, with spur gear ratio of 64:19. Sprague/Thompson-Houston electro-magnetic control. Twelve-shoe pick up. BT-H CP23 compressor. Two Gresham & Craven exhausters. Screw couplings and pockets for buckeye auto-coupler. Power sanding.

Tractive effort: 22,000lb approx.
Brake type: Dual Westinghouse quick-acting system, standard vacuum.

Stock numbering:

Builder	Year	MET Nos
Met-Cam	1907	11-20

Livery:

Similar to 1904 BWE locomotives. Crimson lake body, with black 'mouldings' edged in straw. White lead roof sheets. Solebars crimson lake. Vermilion buffer beams marked 'Met Ry' in gild blocked black. Numbered in 5in gilt characters blocked black. Buffer sockets black with polished steel buffer faces and shanks. All underframe equipment flat dark grey. Two heraldic crests per side. Shoebeams light grey. Headrails, collector shoes and attachment blocks polished steel.

Metropolitan 'Bogie' Steam-Hauled Stock Converted to Electric Working 1906

Electrification to Harrow and Uxbridge in 1905 had resulted in a surplus of 'Bogie' steam-hauled stock. Various proposals were put forward for the propulsion of steam stock by an electric motor car which could be replaced by steam power onward from Harrow. At the same time, the first 'Dreadnought' conversions were taking place, and from the early success of those vehicles it seemed that the 'Bogie' stock would soon be mostly redundant.

One scheme which resulted in two 'Bogie' sets being operated electrically early in 1906 comprised 'down' end propulsion and control from a 1905 single saloon motor car, the return journey being by the same propulsion, but with the control from the 'up' brake end 'Bogie' car which had been adapted for use as a driving trailer. The scheme worked well but the 150 BWE equipment lacked sufficient power for rapid operation.

It was thus decided to fully convert two seven-car sets of 'Bogie' steam-hauled stock (later made up to eight cars) for electric operation, with each set to include two double-equipped motor cars produced from converted former brake-end vehicles using Type 200 BTH equipment. The latter was applied to new Fox 7ft pressed steel motor bogies for use on four double-equipped motor brake coaches. With insufficient space below the floor, control equipments were placed in the original luggage space, and the adjacent passenger compartment was converted for guard and luggage use.

Driving trailers were created by the conversion of the end compartment of an ordinary Second or Third Class car into a driving compartment. Shoe gear was mounted on the trailing bogie.

The first converted set ran on Wednesday, 11 July 1906 on the Uxbridge line. During 1908 a further large number of converted sets were proposed but only two six-car sets fitted with Westinghouse 150 equipment were completed. A proportion of the cars used were from the 1905-06, motor saloon-propelled sets and from the cars used in the earlier 1899-1900 electric traction experiments.

Right:
Driving motor car No 418 on show at the Wembley Exhibition displaying a superb teak and white finish. The revised motor bogies now have spoked wheels of a smaller diameter, with each axle powered by a 150hp traction motor. Originally a Third Class motor car of the 1899 Wembley Park experiment and of 'steam' stock outline, it was rebuilt as a motor car in 1908 to match the earlier 'Bogie' stock conversions. *(U49951)*

Below right:
Ex-'Bogie' steam Third Class trailer No 390 converted as a Driving Trailer for electric operation. Apart from the fitting out of an end compartment with controls, and for control cable runs, the axleboxes were changed for the type to which shoe beams could be attached. It is shown here in varnished teak finish, with panels lined out in Straw and with a grey roof. Long buffers and screw couplings have been fitted to the driving end. *(19203)*

Bottom right:
A seven-car set of 'Bogie' steam stock converted for electric multiple-unit operation. The leading driving motor car, without the lower stepboards, is No 375 which has been downgraded to Third Class from its original Brake Second form. The livery remains the same varnished teak, with white fascia and waist panels. *(U26596)*

Specification:

Original steel underframe, hardwood body, 'Bogie' stock brake end vehicles converted to take four BT-H GE69 200hp traction motors driving new 36in spoked wheels. Traction voltage lighting and heating, Westinghouse compressor and air brake. Later, extra torpedo ventilators fitted above switch compartment. Trailer cars (little altered) coupled by short links, with standard screw coupling and buffing gear at the outer ends of each set. All vehicles featured five-a-side seating with former Second Class accommodation redesignated Third Class.

Compartments: Four in Third Class Motor Coaches (with control equipment in former luggage space, and one former compartment converted for luggage and guard); seven in Third Class trailers; six in First Class Trailers; three First Class and three Third Class in Composite Trailers.

Marshalling: Generally, 3M-3T-1/3T-1T-1/3T-3T-3M (seven-car sets);
3M-3T-3T-1/3T-1T-1/3T-3T-3M (eight-car sets);
3M-3T-3T-1T-3T-3M (six-car sets).
Also known to run as 3M-3T-1/3T-3DT, or in other formations.

Stock numbering:

Conversion date	3DT	3T	1T	1/3T	3M
1905	384*	372/380	364	—	—
1906	387*	392/402	407	—	376/388, 397-398
1906	—	369/373/377	361/408	365/368	—
1906	—	381/393/403	—	412-413	—
1908	—	—	—	—	417-418

* Later converted to Full motor cars.

Livery:

Natural clear varnished teak, with white fascia and waist panels (after 1910 all-teak finish). Roof canvas white lead. Solebars initially painted to simulate teak. Bogie frames and most underframe gear dark grey. Footboards and shoe beams light grey. Heraldic crests on sides. Gilt lettering and numbers, blocked white and blue. Black wheels with white tyres.

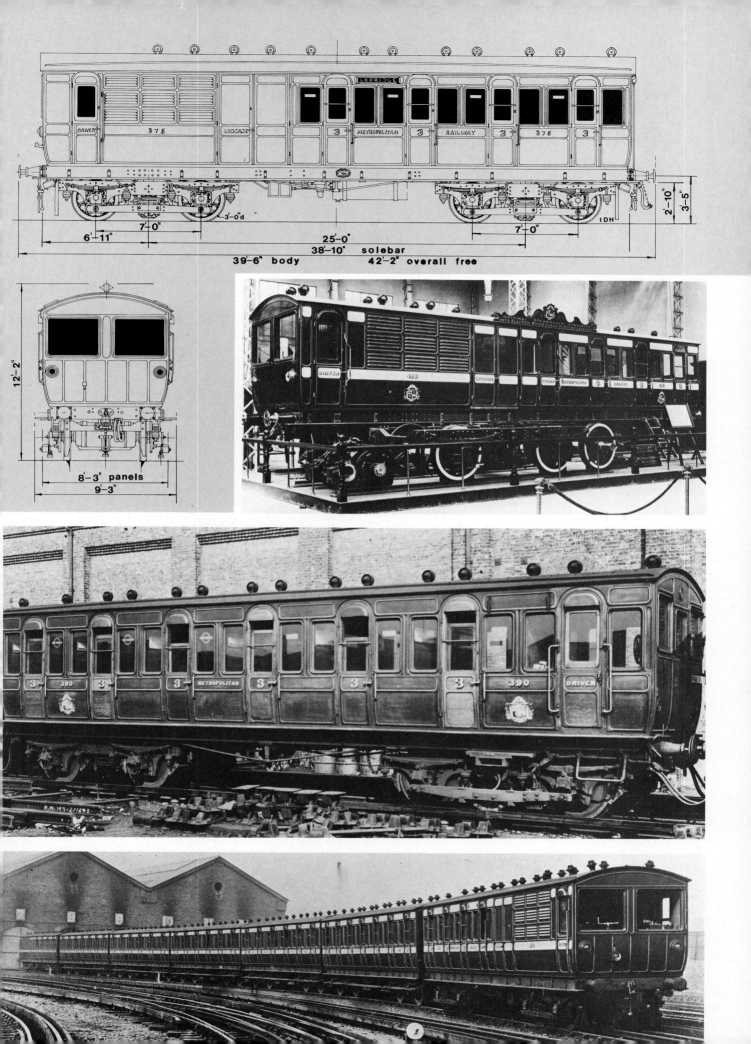

DRIVER 375 LUGGAGE 3 METROPOLITAN 3 RAILWAY 3 375 3

UXBRIDGE

7'-0" 3'-0"d 7'-0" IDH

2'-10"
3'-5"

6'-11" 25'-0"
38'-10" solebar
39'-6" body 42'-2" overall free

12'-2"

8'-3" panels
9'-3"

3 390 3 3 METROPOLITAN 3 3 3 390 DRIVER

Metropolitan Pullman Cars 1909

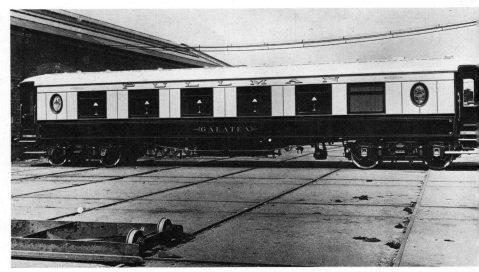

By the early 1900s, the competition offered by Great Central luxury rolling stock was so great that even the First Class vehicles of 'Dreadnought' stock could not prevent main line passengers from deserting the MET. Earlier, in an effort to provide better accommodation, the MET had built two special 32ft First Class six-wheel saloons, for use on the main line. They had been updated in 1905 by conversion into a single 58ft twin saloon bogie vehicle which still could not be compared to the GCR's vestibuled First Class restaurant cars. Thus, in 1909 the MET signed an agreement with the Pullman Car Company for the operation of two cars for a Buffet Service, one each on specially selected main line services.

Built by BRCW, each vehicle seated 19 passengers in armchair luxury in three different sized sections and was equipped with a bar, pantry and lavatory. The interiors had mural panels of fiddle-back mahogany or wainscot oak, inlaid with enrichments to represent a ground of fine quartered veneer. Eight glass-topped tables each had a tiny portable electrolier. Wall bracket lamps were provided, and all fittings including bell pulls and lamp switches were of finely chased and gilded ormolu. Specially woven blinds of green damask were fitted, whilst overhead baggage racks were of ormolu with finely chased ornamentation and panels of brass treillage. Floors were pile carpeted and best morocco covered the armchairs.

The 57ft 3in bodies were constructed on heavy steel underframes fitted with sound deadening material and mounted on 7ft 6in Commonwealth equalised beam bogies with 3ft 4⅝in disc wheels. Automatic vacuum brake and steam heating equipment was fitted, plus standard screw couplings and buffing gear.

An inaugural return trip to Aylesbury was run on Friday, 27 May 1910 with entry into regular traffic following on Wednesday 1 June. The service was finally withdrawn on Saturday 7 October 1939.

Left:
Pullman car *Galatea* in the original standard Pullman umber and cream finish with white roof. *Mayflower* was also in the same finish. Such a scheme was not easy to keep clean, particularly the fine vertically grooved lower side panelling. *(22443)*

Below left:
Galatea seen after both cars had been through a repaint during their 1922/23 overhaul. Overall crimson lake with gilt and straw lining was chosen as the colours stood up well on both steam and electric locomotives. The roof was painted silver grey and the black underframe and bogies were brightened a little by polished axlebox covers. Pullman crests, previously absent, were added — two on each side. *(20709)*

Above:
A close-up of *Mayflower* in crimson livery. On the lower panels only the horizontal lines are painted. The verticals are merely a highlight effect on a sharp edge. Under the name area, the grooves were initially filled and sanded smooth, after which the lettering and lining was then applied. Both cars remained in this livery until they were withdrawn in 1939. *(21567)*

Specification:

Designed by W. S. Laycock & Co and built by BRCW, the cars were of steel underframe and composite body construction, though largely fitted out with hardwood framing and panelling. Equipped for both steam and electric haulage, the first electrically-hauled Pullman cars in Europe. Standard buffers and drawgear. Flexible gangway connections provided for working in pairs. Vacuum braking. Separate dynamo/battery set for electric kitchen equipment.

Stock identification:

Named *Mayflower* and *Galatea*. No numbers.

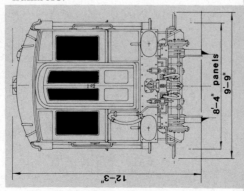

Livery:

Pullman cream and umber, with gilt lining. Gilt lettering with white and blue blocked shading. White roof sheets. Solebar, headstocks, buffer stocks, bogie frames and most underframe gear dark grey. Wheels black with white tyres. Various polished handrails, fittings, buffer heads and shanks. Coloured stained glass used in the oval side lights. (Later a crimson lake livery was used.)

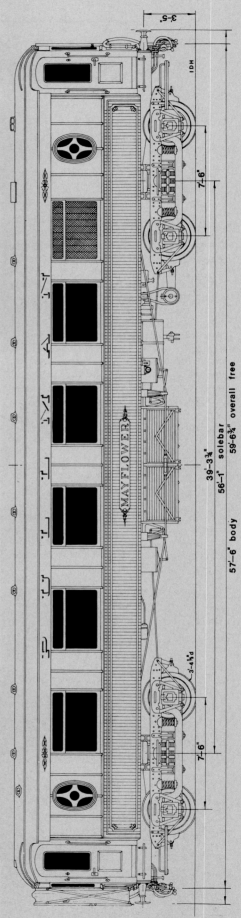

Metropolitan Steam Stock 1910

After the Metropolitan & Great Central Joint service had been operating on the Extension lines for a few years, the gradual introduction of continually improving coaching stock by the latter company began to have an adverse effect on the former's revenue. The GCR main line service included Pullman cars, whilst their restaurant vehicles and other First Class cars were of an almost equivalent standard. In addition, their suburban services were operated with good quality, full length bogie compartment stock which made the Metropolitan's shorter bogie stock look and feel somewhat inferior.

In an attempt to redress the balance, the MET redesigned 10 redundant 1905 electric control trailers to provide conventional compartmentalised bodies, with semi-elliptical roof sections, to suit the original 50ft 10in steel underframes. The reconstruction work was carried out in 1910 by Met-Cam, the end product consisting of two five-car sets comprising All-First, All-Third and Brake Third vehicles. New 7ft pressed steel bogies, at 35ft centres, carrying 36in wheels completely transformed their appearance.

New plush interiors made the trial sets very popular with passengers, even though electric lighting was not initially installed. The Third Class compartments were grouped in threes connected by a narrow central gangway for rapid dispersal of passengers. Steam heating, passenger emergency alarms and standard buffing and coupling gear were fitted.

Later on, the 'semi-open' groups of compartments were found to afford no

particular advantage for passenger movements, and the stock was converted back to a standard layout, a feature retained in all subsequent batches of stock. In 1923 six Brake Thirds were constructed, each having only six compartments and a much larger luggage compartment (as illustrated in the plan).

In 1912 some 20 new cars to the same design were ordered from Met-Cam, with further orders to follow. Some later batches had Stones lighting, and were equipped for haulage by electric locomotives.

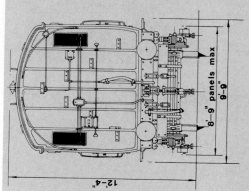

Below left:
A builder's photograph of MET 'Dreadnought' stock Third Class car No 440, as new in 1912 — a traditional style for a more or less traditional form of 'main line' surface railway. The overall varnished teak and hardwood finish was very pleasing, and due to the grade of wood used for the droplight frames, they initially appeared much more bright and golden than the rest of the bodywork. The lining varied subtly from a chrome yellow to a lemon yellow, over a period of years. The lettering and numbering being gilt (or straw) blocked white, with a bright blue shading. *(22442)*

Bottom left:
'Dreadnought' steam stock Brake Third No 492 of a later type. Similar in most respects to the earlier type, this stock was able to adapt for either steam or electric locomotive-hauled services, and formed the backbone of the sets used for country operations. *G. Kichenside*

Bottom right:
1920 'Dreadnought' Brake Third No 485, equipped for both steam and electric haulage. For the latter, shoe gear was carried for the collection of current for heating and lighting purposes. The electric locomotives had dual braking systems, thus the vacuum-equipped coaching stock did not require the fitting of the Westinghouse brake. It was known as 'steam' stock in order to differentiate it from similarly styled stock operating in multiple-unit 'MV' and 'MW' trains. *(H/16176)*

Specification:

Rolled steel channel and angle underframe, hardwood framed and panelled body with semi-elliptical roof and torpedo ventilation. Fox type pressed steel bogies. Pintsch high-pressure lighting. Emergency alarm and automatic vacuum brake. Laycock steam heating. Single full-length footboards were fitted to the solebars immediately below the side panelling.

Compartments: Seven in All-Firsts; nine in All-Thirds, arranged in groups of three; by B3 arranged in groups of 3+3+1, or 2+3+2. First Class compartments, with Lincrusta ceilings and inlaid linoleum floors, provided four-a-side seating upholstered with plush moquette and equipped with folding armrests. Third Class compartments, with millboard ceilings and inlaid cork flooring, offered five-a-side seating with Terry upholstery. All compartments were fitted with spring roller blinds and incandescent mantles.

Marshalling: B3-3-1-1-B3 (five-car sets)
B3-3-1-1-3-B3 (six-car sets).

Stock numbering:

Builder	Year	1T	3T	B3
Met-Cam	1910	419-422	423-424	425-428
Met-Cam	1912	429-436	437-440	441-448
Met-Cam	1920	449-462	463-476	477-490

Livery:

Natural clear varnished teak. Lined out in straw. Gilt lettering and numbering, blocked white and blue. Roof canvas white lead. Solebars and all underframe gear, bogie sideframes dark grey. Wheels black, tyres white. Two full colour heraldic crests per side. Light grey footboards. After about 1953, the outer ends of Brake Thirds were painted vermilion.

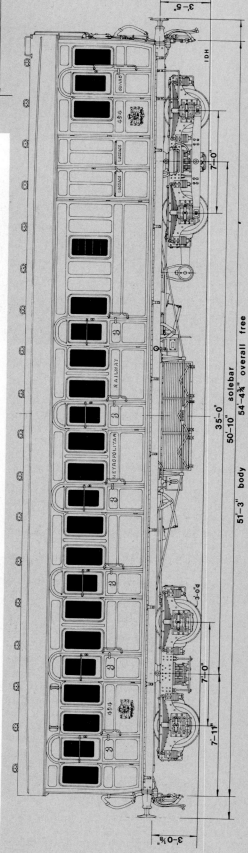

District 'E' Stock 1914

This stock was the last batch to be produced as a result of the 1909-10 expansion programme. The cars were constructed by the Gloucester Railway Carriage & Wagon Co to the same basic body style as the 'C' and 'D' stock, but for the first time incorporated an elliptical roof section in place of the long used Monitor style. The new roof line followed main line railway practice and in similar vein was fitted initially with Laycock torpedo ventilators. They proved too effective in service on open stock, which featured extensive fan light ventilation, and were subsequently removed. For this stock new heavier plate frame motor and trailer bogies were introduced, the lighter pressed steel units on the 'C' and 'D' stock having already caused problems.

After 1918, some of the earlier 'B' stock units were updated, and during a three-year period all stock apart from the 'A' vehicles was modified to provide total interchangeability with other stock. This enabled any formation to be coupled up according to availability and duty requirements. Motor bogie problems continued, and various interim designs were tried whilst repairs were carried out. Many bogies were interchanged, thus stock could appear very mixed, and in many cases newer style bogies were built and fitted to over 50 of the older cars.

This order was for what was hoped to be the forerunner of a fleet of stream-lined sets. The motor cars, of which the order was largely composed, were to be followed at later dates by further batches of similarly-styled trailer cars, so that the earlier all-wooden cars

could be withdrawn. However, the intervention of World War 1 brought a halt to that particular expansion scheme, and the 'E' stock became an integral part of the mixed 'B', 'C' and 'D' stocks.

Various items of reconditioned 'C', 'D' and 'E' stock survived into LPTB days,

although all retained hand-worked doors and were eventually redesignated as 'H' stock. Many saw several more years of service after Nationalisation in 1948 before being finally withdrawn in stages as new 'R38', 'R47' and 'R49' stock was introduced.

Top:
Gloucester-built 1914 'E' stock motor car No 275 photographed in April 1920, and showing some signs of wear. Less rigid than the preceding 'C' and 'D' stock and not as heavy, it did not ride as well as expected. Note destination board and 'not stopping at' rack at the trailing end. By this date all cars were being repainted with a brighter scarlet finish at times of overhaul, although the doors still remained in the darker 'mahogany' finish. *(U5808)*

Above:
'E' stock had pleasing lines as this photographed shows and was the first MDR stock to have a non-clerestory roof. An advantage was that both motor car and trailer car bodies were identical, including the end compartments. Conversion of motor cars to trailers and vice versa of a later date was expected, but due to the short life of the stock it did not take place. Those cars which survived were marshalled in later life in 'H' stock trains. *(U55860)*

Top:
Trailer car No 568 at Ealing Common depot around 1920. Problems were experienced with over-ventilation via the roof shell units during cold weather. Later these were blocked off, and later still were removed altogether. Note the very light pressed-steel trailer bogies and very small wheels, factors which did not help the riding qualities of the stock, which greatly deterioriated after some five years of service. This fact caused the MDR to consider the possibilities of introducing all-steel bodies for their next order for stock. *(41261)*

Above:
A 1913 'E' stock motor car on District Line service. Very similar in basic construction to the 'C' and 'D' classes, the cars appeared rather squat due to the very smooth and low roof line. This was the first Underground stock to appear with a plain elliptical-section roof with rounded ends, and fears were expressed that this form of roof would not provide enough rigidity for a car with such an open structure. These anxieties proved to be unfounded, although the style was not liked by the mechanical engineers. *Ian Allan Library*

Specification:

Steel underframe. Body largely hardwood framed but with composite panelling. New elliptical roof section. Initial ventilation by Laycock torpedo vents on roof. Motor cars single equipped with plate frame 'C' type motor bogie with two GE212 traction motors with interpoles. Plate frame 'M' type trailer bogie. BT-H non-automatic electro-magnetic control. All motor cars carried compressors. Westinghouse automatic brake.

Layout: Open saloon form with all cars offering 48 or 52 seats with the use of occasional seating.

Marshalling: All cars were interchangeable on duty, thus formations varied.

Stock numbering:

Builder	Year	3M	3T
Gloucester	1914	258-283	565-568

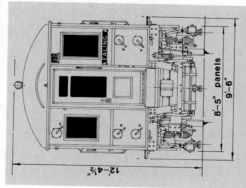

Livery:

Medium scarlet body. Crimson lake fascia and solebar. Window and door frames stained and laquered dark maroon and/or enamelled in crimson lake. White lead roof sheets. Gilt numbering, blocked white and blue. Bogie frames and underframe gear dark grey. Black wheels and tyres. Light grey shoebeam. Wartime shortages limited the use of a brighter scheme. Several livery changes followed at intervals.

Metropolitan Electric Stock 1913/1919

Rapid expansion of the MET following through running once more of Baker Street on the Extension Lines required further rolling stock, and from running over the East London Railway. In 1913 orders were placed with Met-Cam for 23 motor cars and 20 trailers which were nearly identical in size and design to the 1905-06 saloon stock, differing only in having an elliptical section roof. A reshuffle of electrical equipment sets resulted in the acquisition of 13 new BWE sets, and to the use of 10 BT-H sets recovered from the 1907 locomotives. The stock ran mainly on the Circle Line and East London service, much of it mixed and integrated with the earlier saloon stock. The interruption of developments by World War 1 allowed some thought to be applied to future stock design and some experimental conversions were subsequently carried out by Met-Cam. The main idea was to try and get a compromise between compartment and saloon stock.

In 1919 an earlier six-car set of BWE 150 saloon stock was chosen for conversion. This work involved the fitting of an elliptical roof and four slam doors per side to the Motor Thirds. Five similar doors were fitted to each side of the Trailer Thirds. The motor cars retained the usual luggage compartment but passenger access was available to part of it for rush hour use, and the dividing bulkhead between it and the main passenger compartment had windows inserted so that any luggage could be observed. The Third Class Trailer cars had different seating layouts. One had 'regular' door pitching, the other was divided into several variably sized seating areas so that the doors were not regularly spaced. First Class Driving Trailers had a driving compartment with doors; on each side of the vehicle there were five passenger doors. Initially gangway doors were provided at the driving ends only. Later they were provided throughout.

A further innovation was the placing of all heating and lighting switches for the whole train under the control of the guards as opposed to the then normal practice of fitting each car with separate switches. Electric windscreen wiping was provided.

The train itself worked well, the only minor problem being a degree of confusion and congestion caused by the large number of narrow doors which resulted in some passenger indecision as to which door to use. Such door spacing and design was not therefore used again.

Below:
One of the 1905 BWE 150 electric cars rebuilt as First Class Driving Trailer No 55 for the 'Hustler' train. All of the converted cars followed a similar body style under an elliptical roof form. The motor cars included the customary luggage compartment behind the driver, leaving space for only four swing doors per side. *(22454)*

Specification:

Conversions on 1905 BWE 150 steel underframed stock. New elliptical section roof. New hardwood framing and upper panelling, with sheet brass and steel lower panelling with multiple slam-door layout. Motor cars retained the BWE 150 equipment and the small luggage compartment. BWE electro-pneumatic 'turret' control. Westinghouse automatic brake.

Layout: Semi-open saloon form, with windscreens at door positions. Third Class Motors and Trailer Cars seated 41 and 58 respectively. First Class Driving Trailers seated 44.

Marshalling: Generally 3M-3T-1DT+1DT-3T-3M, though many mixed formations with earlier saloon motor cars.

Livery:

Natural clear varnished teak with simulated painted teak on metal panels. White lead roof canvas. Solebars, bogie frame and most underframe equipment dark grey. Footboards and shoebeams light grey. Heraldic crests on sides. Gilt lettering and numbering blocked white and blue. Black wheels and white tyres.

Stock numbering:

The experimental converted 'Hustle' train retained its original numbers.

Builder	Year	3M	1DT	3T
Met-Cam	1919	36/44*	53/55	35/67

* Converted in 1936 to trailer cars and renumbered 197 and 198. 'Hustler' train then ran as an eight-car set between 'MW' stock motor cars.

Metropolitan 'H' Class 4-4-4T 1920

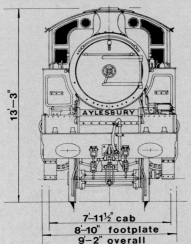

13'-3"

7'-11½" cab
8'-10" footplate
9'-2" overall

As soon as possible following the peace of 1918, the MET set about a massive improvement of its 'country' services. Charles Jones designed a handsome looking 4-4-4T to which was given the classification 'H'.

Production of the locomotives was placed with Kerr, Stuart & Co — four leaving the works in 1920, and a further four early in 1921. Although similar in superstructure to the 'G' class locomotives, the 'H', with 19in×26in out-

Above:
MET Class H 4-4-4T No 106 in works photographic grey finish. *LPC (5116)*

Right:
An interesting comparison of MET traction forms. Although similarly liveried, lettered and lined out, electric Bo-Bo No 19 looks very streamlined when compared with Charles Jones' Class H 4-4-4T. The partial drawback of electric traction was that it did not cover the entire MET system. On the Extension Lines, electric track extended at first only to Harrow, though later the change of motive power was made at Rickmansworth. *Ian Allan Library*

Below right:
A right-hand side view of Class H No 103 taken shortly after it had entered traffic, before the front footplate hand rails had been added. *LPC (1484)*

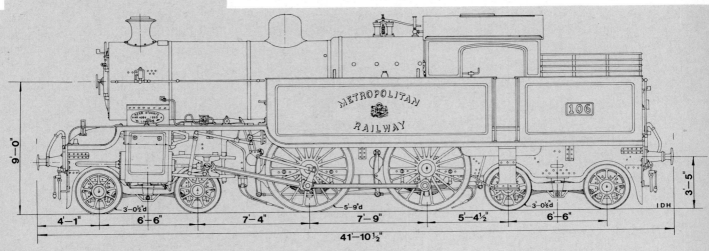

9'-0"

3'-5"

4'-1"   6'-6"   7'-4"   7'-9"   5'-4½"   6'-6"
3'-0½"d   5'-9"d   3'-0½"d
41'-10½"

side cylinders and Walschaerts valve gear, looked far more elegant in operation, even though the new wheel arrangement produced slightly less tractive effort.

Most of the previous MET locomotive characteristics, such as the heavily waisted chimney, small round dome cover and oval buffers were retained, but new features were footsteps on the front and rear bufferbeams, curved top handrails on the front of the smokebox and (fitted shortly after entering service) a pair of curved handrails running from the front bufferbeam to the front edge of the raised running plate.

Three destination plates could be carried one behind the other in large brackets raised above the mainframes just in front of the smoke box door and the usual multitude of lamp brackets were fitted, due to the variety of codes needed for work over the electrified sections of the line. A large coal bunker capacity and two large side tanks ensured that non-stop 'express' working could be maintained.

Wheelslip could be easily achieved when opening up for a quick start on wet rails, but running was fast and smooth and the locomotives would appear to have been well-liked by their crews. In 1935 all eight of these locomotives were handed over to the LNER becoming reclassified as 'H2'.

Specification:

Non-condensing, superheated side tank locomotive. Inside frames, with two 19in×26in outside cylinders. Piston valves with Walschaerts valve gear. Belpaire firebox and Ramsbottom safety valves.

Heating area: Tubes 1,046sq ft, firebox 132sq ft, superheater 180sq ft, total 1,358sq ft.

Grate area: 21.2sq ft.

Boiler pressure: 160lb/sq in.

Tractive effort: 17,400lb approximately.

Water capacity: 2,000gal.

Coal capacity: 4ton 10cwt.

Stock numbering:

Year	MET Nos	Works Nos	LNER Nos
1920	103-106	4088-91	6415-6418
1921	107*-110	4092-95	6419-6422

* On the original large works plate 107 was dated 1920.

Livery:

Boiler cladding, tanks, cab, bunker and footplate valance, footsteps, cylinder cladding, dome and wheels all crimson lake. Boiler, tanks and bunker lined out in black, edged with straw. Valance straw lined. Inner edges of tyres and axle ends thinly lined in straw. Black smokebox, chimney and footplate. Frames and other items below footplate black. Vermilion buffer beams edged in black and fine lined in straw. Gilt and/or straw numbering and lettering — some blocked with white and blue. Cast brass number plates infilled with vermilion. Polished steel connecting and coupling rods, slide bars, valve gear, piston valve and cylinder cover plates, smokebox door hinges, fittings and handrails, buffer heads and shanks.

District 'F' Stock 1920

After World War 1, the District Railway evolved several all-steel design layouts for improved 'E' stock. It was felt that end doors caused delays in that entraining passengers could only go in one direction, whereas with centre doors they went in two directions and dispersed quickly. Metal working required the use of duplicated parts for ease of construction, so a design soon evolved where the basic trailer car was equipped with three sets of identical double doors (running on ball bearings) equally spaced out on each side; for the first time the continuous footboard was dispensed with. The doors were in fact only metal framed and were infilled with hardwood panelling (though in later life they had to be replaced with light-alloy).

The body width was increased by 11in, making the overall width 9ft 7in. Built on a steel underframe 49ft 8¼in long over the headstocks, the motor car bodies only differed from those of the trailers in the fitting of single side doors at each end for the driver and guard respectively, in place of the last window unit. Even the car ends were common, all having a pair of elliptical windows either side of a central gangway door.

Design for speedy operation (up to 45mph), the motor cars were double-equipped on heavy plate-frame bogies of 13ft overall length. A semi-elliptical roof was adopted, into which six ventilators of a new type were set. The latter worked too well and were soon sealed up. Outside, all metal fittings were either bronze or of nickel-plated steel; inside, all steel work, panelling and mouldings were painted to resemble teak. The steel floor was linoleum-covered, while the ceiling was of moulded asbestos millboard into which were set numerous lamps in double and single fittings. Some 20 heaters were placed behind perforated front plates beneath the seats.

The 12 'F' stock trains (with four spare motor cars), were long lived, were modified several times, and successfully tested several experimental equipments.

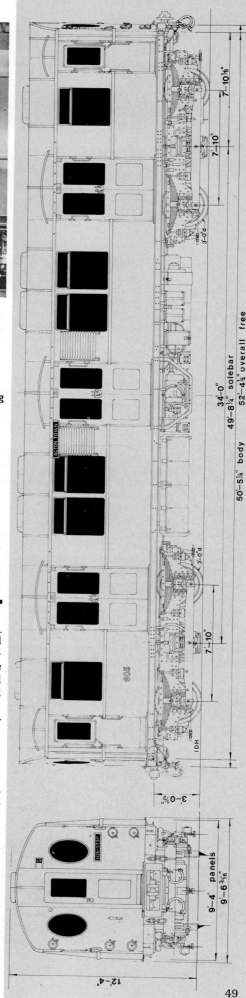

Far left:
A MDR 'F' stock train, originally built by Met-Cam in 1920, but much modified during later years. The leading car (LPTB No 4640) is a former control trailer converted to a single-equipped driving motor car and as such has no guard's position. Motor bogies and equipments were from the scrapped MDR electric locomotives. *(U47548)*

Left:
A post-World War 1 MDR 'F' stock train, shown here fitted with trip cocks. The leading car is No 601. The livery is plain and may reflect the shortages felt very much at that time. It is alleged to be in a non-standard 'lake' (a colour falling somewhere between crimson and scarlet), doors included, and lacks the contrasting waist rail and other colourings. The roof is a plain darkish grey. *(U61)*

Below left:
'F' stock trailer No 8522 post 1938, after provision with air-worked doors. The stock apart from being the MDR's first all-steel design, has been the only surface stock to have elliptical windows at the car ends, including the driver's look out. *(U57491)*

Above:
A close up of motor car No 601, showing hand-operated sliding doors, 'not stopping at' station plates and part of the underfloor equipment with opened access panels. The whole of the body side, including the doors appears to be painted a single colour — possibly 'non-standard Lake'. From the solebars down all appears to be black. *(U65)*

Specification:

All steel underframed and bodied stock. Full elliptical roof section with grouped 'dome' ventilation. Steel door frames, hardwood panelled. Motor cars double-equipped with four GE260 traction motors with tapped field system on heavy plate framed Type 'E' bogies. Spur gear ratio 19:64. Trailer cars fitted with plate framed Type 'N' bogies. BT-H electro-magnetic control, with hand notching of individual contactors. Hand operated doors. Westinghouse compressors and Type 20 brake.

Layout: Semi-open saloons. Motor cars seating 40, control trailers 44 and all other trailers 48.

Marshalling: 3M-3T-1/3T-3T-3M+1/3CT-3T-3M, or similar.

Stock numbering:

The initial numbering was retained for some while in spite of several overall stock changes, and was not altered under the numbering revisions of 1920-23.

Builder	Year	3M	1/3CT	1/3T	3T
Met-Cam	1920	600-639	900-911	1000-1011	1012-1135

Livery:

Supplied in dark crimson lake, unlined and unlettered due to wartime/postwar restrictions; 'grotesque' car numbers (one set per car). White roof. Solebar, headstocks, bogies and all underframe equipment dark grey. Polished axlebox covers. Light grey shoebeams. Later adopted bright scarlet over all bodywork except doors, with black waist rail. Brighter standard schemes followed at intervals.

Metropolitan Electric Stock 1921

Production cars resulting from the 1919 'Hustler' train experiment followed closely the body styles of both that train set and the previous 1913 stock. The 1921 design sought less seats but bigger entrance vestibules and central gangways. Essentially, the trailer cars employed three sets of 4ft wide sliding doors per side. These entered service first, running with 1913 motor cars on the Inner Circle Line, where they proved an instant success. As before, end gangway doors were not provided. A small number of Driving Trailer Firsts followed and subsequently the 1921 motor cars were introduced. They had the usual small luggage compartment, from which a narrow pair of double doors opened into the passenger compartment. Two pairs of 4ft wide sliding doors, identical to those on the trailer cars, were fitted on each side of the passenger compartment. One consequence of the similarities between the 1913 and 1921 stock is that bogies and traction equipment would appear to have been exchanged between them at various times. Also trains of mixed stock were frequently used.

Traction equipment for this stock, as on the 1913 stock, was not all new, since bogies and control equipments were from the original electric locomotives, then undergoing a total rebuild to take Metropolitan-Vickers*

equipments (1922). All motor cars had similar 200 BWE equipments and all motor bogies had 86M traction motors, but by virtue of the two different bogie side-frame forms and wheelbase lengths, the stock was divided into two classes.

During 1933-34, all of the 1913-21 stock was overhauled and regrouped for Circle Line working. A mixture of traction equipment was employed from other displaced stock, and body modifications included the installation of end gangway doors. All seating was re-upholstered, the general aim being to

parallel as closely as possible the standards of the more modern District stock. The 1913 stock vehicles could be easily identified by their double centre and single end-doors on each side and double waist rail. The 1921 stock had three pairs of double doors per side and a single waist rail.

* British Westinghouse Electrical and Manufacturing Co's (BWE) electrical interests were taken over by Metropolitan Vickers Electrical Co Ltd during 1919. This was a separate entity from the Westinghouse Brake and Signal Co.

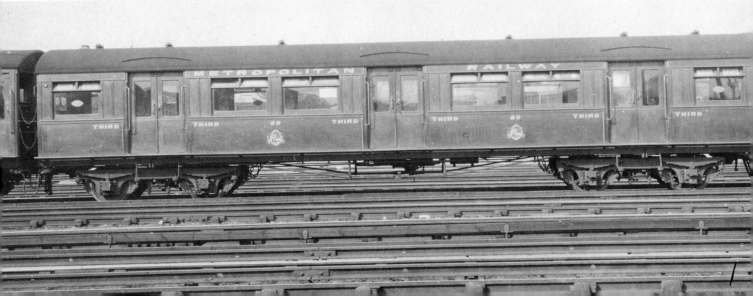

Below left:
MET 1921 stock motor car No 117, built by Met-Cam with 7ft 9in bogies and BWE 86M 200hp traction motors. The car is seen in original form with luggage compartment and varnished teak finish. *LPC (10850)*

Bottom left:
MET 1921 Third Class trailer No 89. Three sets of double sliding doors per side made for rapid and easy access, yet there was much hesitation by the Board of Directors to run this form of car layout anywhere other than on the Inner Circle. The stock was of pleasant appearance and rode well, but the design was not to be repeated. *LPC (10849)*

Below:
A MET 1921 stock train at South Kensington on a Circle Line working after the motor cars had the luggage compartment replaced with seats, and end centre doors had been fitted to all cars. Leading car (LPTB No 2579) is shown in the modern all scarlet finish of the 1950s whilst on Circle Line working. *(1795)*

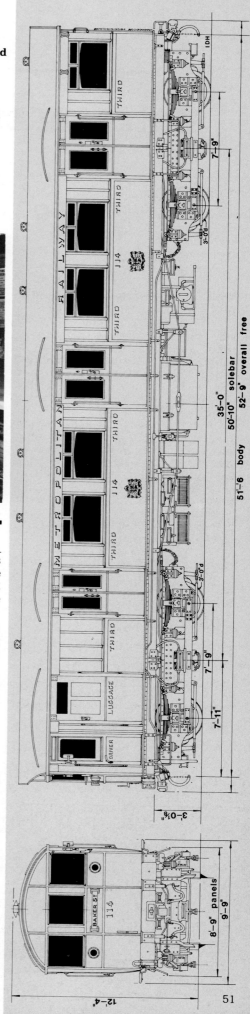

Specification:

Steel underframe, with hardwood body frames and upper panelling. Sheet brass and steel lower panelling. Elliptical roof section. Bogies were taken from the electric locomotives Nos 1-20. All had BWE 86M 200hp traction motors and BWE electro-pneumatic 'turret' control. Half the bogies were of 7ft 6in wheelbase, the other half 7ft 9in. Fitted with Westinghouse compressor and automatic brake.

Layout: Semi-open saloons, with internal glass partitions at door positions. The 1913 stock seating was as follows: Motor Thirds 38; Trailer Thirds 48; Driving Trailer Firsts 48. The 1921 stock seated 37 in Motor Thirds, 50 in Trailer Thirds and 45 in Driving Trailer Firsts (divided into smoking and non-smoking).

Marshalling: Mixed stock formations of 1913-21 (and some 1905-06 stock), arranged in four-car sets for Circle Line working; later made up to five-car sets. After 1933/34 re-conditioning they still remained as five-car sets. Examples are:

3M-3T-3T-1DT
3M-3T-1DT-3T-3M.

Stock numbering:

Builder	Year	3M	3T	1DT
Met-Cam	1913	83- 92 (BT-H)*	77- 86	77-86
Met-Cam	1913	93-105 (BWE)†	—	—
Met-Cam	1921	106-125 (BWE)‡	87-119	87/92

* 7ft 6in bogies from 1906 electric locomotives.
† 7ft 9in bogies (new).
‡ 7ft 6in and 7ft 9in bogies from scrapped 1904 and 1906 electric locomotives.

Livery:

Standard, natural varnished teak with lower metal panels painted, grained and stippled to simulate teak. White lead roof canvas. Gilt lettering and numbering, blocked white and blue. Solebars, bogie frames and most underframe equipment dark grey. Footboards and shoebeams light grey. Black wheels and white tyres.

Metropolitan Electric Locomotive 1921

In 1919 a postwar appraisal of the MET rolling stock, deemed that the quite successful BT-H electric locomotives of 1906 should be re-equipped with more powerful motors. To do that, the empty body shell required an increase in length, as it was felt necessary to fit heavy-duty plate-framed bogies, equipped with wheels of as large a diameter as possible, each with double brake blocks. As there had been some complaints from drivers about the occurrence of wind noise under certain conditions on the flat fronted locos, a new style of 'blunt vee' nose was considered. Better internal ventilation was also required, as was improved access to new equipments. Since the

Below:
MET Bo-Bo No 9 *John Milton* **in an early livery and wearing the original form of cast name plate attached during 1928. The plate replaced the 'METROPOLITAN' lettering although the full colour heraldic emblems remained. The vermilion solebar shows up well against the darker crimson lake body.** *(U13920)*

Above right:
Bo-Bo No 18 *Michael Faraday* **in very late life and livery. The nameplates were removed during World War 2, but were eventually replaced in cast aluminium. The paint scheme became less complicated, with the roof painted red oxide and the body dark maroon with the simplest of straw lining. Buffer beams and solebars were all vermilion, with black bogies and underframe gear, relieved only with light grey shoe beams.** *(778)*

Far right:
Bo-Bo No 19 in original livery. *Ian Allan Library*

Right:
Bo-Bo No 14 with an 'express' for Chesham. The third car of the train is one of the two MET Pullman coaches, and the rest of the train is comprised of compartmented 'Dreadnought' steam stock adapted for electric locomotive haulage. *LPC (1955M)*

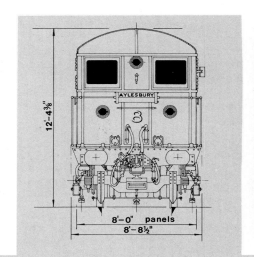

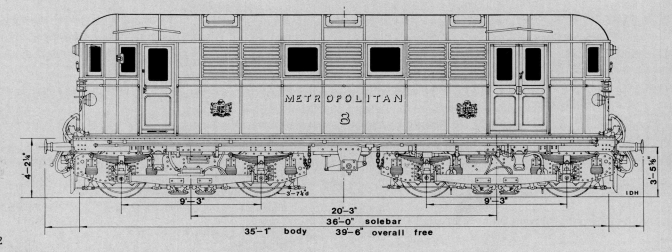

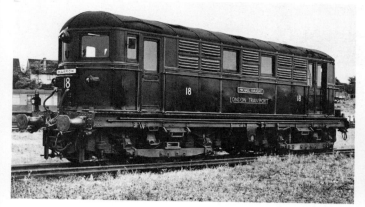
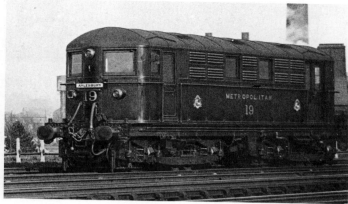
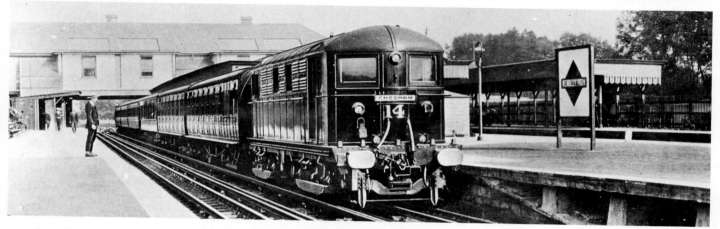

supply of the earlier locomotives, Metropolitan-Vickers Ltd had taken over British Westinghouse and the successors arranged for their massive MV339 traction motors and new electro-magnetic control equipment to form the basis of the new design.

The actual rebuilding was a massive task but only one of the original 10 BWE locos, and one of the 10 BT-H locos were to re-emerge in revised form. So much work went into the first conversions that a decision was made to scrap the remainder and an entirely new set of bodies were constructed.

Although screw couplings were fitted as standard, mountings for buckeye couplings were provided so that the locomotive could haul similarly fitted multiple-unit stock in an emergency. Dual braking with heavy duty rigging was fitted, and all equipments in the body were set along the centreline of the vehicle giving good access from either side. With much more satisfactory driving positions at each end with fully duplicated controls, and all switch panels, contactors and resistance banks mounted on racks over the centralised equipments, the new locomotives were highly suited to rapid acceleration and retardation as well as to high-speed running on the open sections of the Extension lines. In service their performance equalled, if not excelled, the best of the MET 'express' steam locomotives.

Specification:

Steel underframe with steel framed and panelled main body. Steel framed hardwood doors. Wood window framing. Heavy plate-framed steel bogies with four MV339 300hp traction motors with spur gearing ratio 23:57. MET-VICK electro-magnetic control gear. Twelve-shoe current pick-up. Two Gresham & Craven exhausters (some fitted with Reavell RB8 rotary exhausters). Screw and/or buck-eye couplings.

Tractive effort: 22,600lb approximately.

Brake type: Westinghouse (originally with 8G2 compressor), Standard vacuum.

Stock numbering:

As delivered in 1921-23 all had large painted numerals on nose and sides. In 1927 all were additionally named and carried cast brass plates on each side of the body. There were two changes of name however, at later stages.

Builder	Year	Met No	Met Name	Met No	Met Name
Vickers Ltd	(1921-1923)	1	John Lyon	11	George Romney
Vickers Ltd	(1921-1923)	2	Oliver Cromwell*	12	Sarah Siddons
Vickers Ltd	(1921-1923)	3	Sir Ralph Verney	13	Dick Whittington
Vickers Ltd	(1921-1923)	4	Lord Byron	14	Benjamin Disraeli
Vickers Ltd	(1921-1923)	5	John Hampden	15	Wembley 1924
Vickers Ltd	(1921-1923)	6	William Penn	16	Oliver Goldsmith†
Vickers Ltd	(1921-1923)	7	Edmund Burke	17	Florence Nightingale†
Vickers Ltd	(1921-1923)	8	Sherlock Holmes	18	Michael Faraday
Vickers Ltd	(1921-1923)	9	John Milton†	19	John Wycliffe†
Vickers Ltd	(1921-1923)	10	William Ewart Gladstone‡	20	Sir Christopher Wren†

* Later Lord Thomas   † Nameplates not replaced after the war   ‡ Later W. E. Gladstone

Livery:

As delivered, crimson lake (deep scarlet) body including doors, with black 'mouldings' edged in straw. Light grey roof sheets. Solebars crimson lake. Plain vermilion buffer beams and sockets, with polished steel buffer faces and shanks. Footplate and all gear below frame black. Plain stained and varnished window frames. Two heraldic crests per side. Straw numerals (9in) and lettering (5in). Bright brass polished headlamp cases. Polished steel handrails, collector shoes and attachment blocks. Light grey shoebeams. Several livery changes followed.

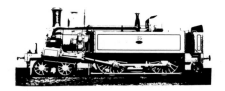

District 'G' Stock 1923

By 1922 much of the earlier wooden-bodied multiple unit stock needed either scrapping or major overhaul. The economic solution appeared to be to scrap life-expired trailer cars and replace them with converted former motor cars, thereby enabling a batch of new motor cars to be constructed. By exchanging the various motors and old equipments, the new stock would be compatible with the old, particularly if both the old cast steel and interim light plate-frame motor bogies were replaced with a much stronger plate-frame design. Fifty 'G' class motor cars constructed by Gloucester were of composite steel and wood form in order to have some similarity in operational use to the older wooden stock it was to run with.

The body structure below the cant rail was similar to that of the all-steel 'F' stock, although the sides were vertical. Only two pairs of double sliding doors were installed on each side, in addition to the end doors for the driver and guard. As before, the driver's compartment was for his occupancy only, and both end areas were very much narrower than before. This layout provided much more space for passenger circu-

Above:
An interesting photograph exposing much of the underfloor equipment carried by 'G' stock driving motor car No 4248, as it was eased into the LT Museum at Covent Garden on Sunday 20 May 1979. *(1044/A9)*

Below:
A 'Q23' stock train of the mid-1960s. The leading motor car, No 4248, is now preserved in the LT Museum. With an overhaul date of March 1965 this car is in the final all-scarlet livery of 'London Transport', with the underframe and all associated fittings black, apart from the light grey shoebeams. *(H/16131)*

lation in the main compartment. The roof style reverted to the old raised central portion though strangely without the rounded downswept ends. Efforts were made to reduce the thickness of window and door frame reveals giving a pleasing, almost flush-sided look to the cars. Doors for the driver and guard were of the hinged variety.

A significant aspect of the entry into traffic of the 'G' class motor cars was the introduction of the 7ft 10in wheelbase 'A2' heavy plate-frame motor bogie, and a similar but more lightly constructed 7ft 3in wheelbase 'K2' trailer bogie. Both designs proved highly satisfactory, being very reliable and almost maintenance free. The combination of these bogies and the 'G' class body set a standard of basic car design that was to continue for over a decade.

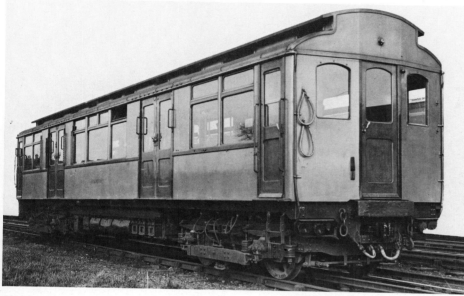

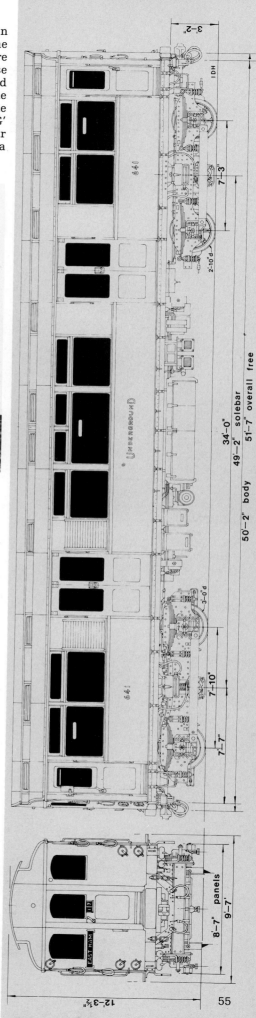

Above:
This 'G' stock motor car displays a quantity of useful detail. The colour scheme is basic 'Underground', with scarlet body and the darker crimson lake doors. The waistrail and verticals alongside each doorway are black, as is all solebar and underframe equipment. The shoebeams and bogies, once light grey, have assumed a brownish coating of mud and brake dust. The overhaul date appears to be February 1924. The driving end is furthest from the camera. *(23875)*

Specification:

Steel underframe. Composite steel and hardwood body framing, with sheet steel panelling. Plain clerestory steel roof with louvred ventilation. New plate-frame 'A2' motor bogie fitted with earlier 1905 BT-H GE69 200hp traction motors. BT-H electro-magnetic control. New plate-frame 'K2' type trailer bogies. All cars equipped with Westinghouse brake and compressor. Double block rigged brakes.

Layout: Semi-open saloon seating 44 as Third Class motor cars.

Marshalling: Usually ran in mixed sets of older trailer cars, with an equal number of motors to trailers.
Examples, early forms:
M-T-T-M-M-T-T-M
M-T-T-M-M-T-M.
Examples, later forms:
M-T-T-M-T-M-T-M
M-T-T-M-T-M.

Livery:

These vehicles saw the reintroduction of the brighter scarlet scheme, as tried briefly in 1914. Scarlet body, with crimson lake solebars, cant rail strip, doors and window frames and the vertical section of the clerestory. Light grey roof sheets. All underframe equipment, including bogies, black. Light grey shoebeams.

Stock numbering:

Followed on the sequence from 'F' stock motor cars:

Builder	Year	MDR Nos
Gloucester	1923	640-679
Gloucester	1923	800-809

In 1928 all were renumbered as follows:
230-294 (Even Nos only westbound)
295-327 (Odd Nos only eastbound)

Later on, rigged to operate directionally, ie 33 west-facing and 17 east-facing.

Metropolitan 'K' Class 2-6-4T 1924

Above:
A view of Class K 2-6-4T No 111 showing its very pleasing lines. The design was not to be confused with the SECR 'River' class tank locomotive but rather with the much earlier 2-6-0 and 2-6-4T designs for war locomotives produced by Maunsell in 1917. War surplus 'Mogul' parts were reworked into a tank design by George Hally, and with postwar economy in mind, the original livery was scheduled to be black overall with plain straw lettering and lined. *Ian Allan Library*

With the MET still following a progressive expansion of its post-World War 1 improvement programme, a need arose for a powerful mixed traffic locomotive, mainly for work on the increasing freight traffic that was being generated during the early 1920s. Some preliminary design work by George Hally was already in progress during

1921, when many wartime locomotive parts were on offer from the government's Railway Operating Division (ROD).

As it was, the Ministry of Munitions had placed an order for 100 Moguls (2-6-0 tender locomotives) with Woolwich Arsenal — this being one effective type needed by all the peace-

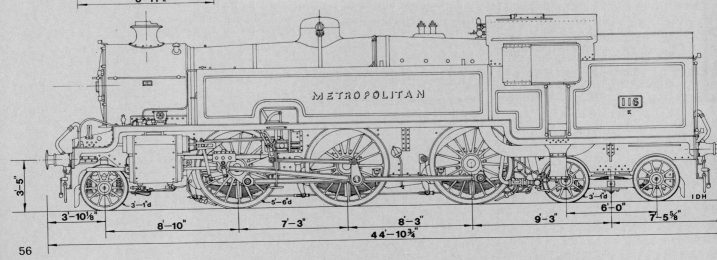

time railway companies. The Mogul design (in this case by R. E. L. Maunsell) had evolved under the wartime authority of the Association of Railway Locomotive Engineers and the ROD, and appeared in 1917 as the SECR prototype No 810 (later to become SECR Class N). Maunsell had also designed a 2-6-4T locomotive, using similar parts and numbered 790 (to be developed later still as the SECR 'River' class tank). Although some of the Arsenal Moguls were purchased, most of the parts were sold to George Cohen and the Armstrong Disposal Corporation, who re-offered the parts at a lower price.

It was at that stage that Hally could see the parts coming together in a tank design similar to Maunsell's No 790 and therefore an order was placed with Armstrong Whitworth to gather sufficient parts suited to the construction of six locomotives. Unlike Maunsell's 'River' class, the MET Class K 2-6-4T was a great success, even though it was limited to working only the surface sections of the extension lines.

Like the Class H locomotives, they later passed into LNER ownership as Class L2.

Specification:

Non-condensing, superheated, mixed traffic side tank locomotive. Piston valves with Walschaerts valve gear, Belpaire firebox and Ross safety valves. Inside frames, two 19in×28in outside cylinders,

Heating area: Tubes 1,372.6sq ft, firebox 135sq ft, superheater 285sq ft, total 1,792.6sq ft.

Grate area: 25sq ft.

Boiler pressure: 200lb/sq in.

Water capacity: 2,000gal.

Coal capacity: 4 tons.

Tractive effort: 24,400lb approx.

Brake type: Vacuum.

Stock numbering:

Year	Met Nos	LNER Nos
1924	111-116	6158-6163

Livery:

Boiler cladding, tank, cab, bunker and footplate valance, footsteps, cylinder cladding, dome and wheels all crimson lake. Boiler, tanks and bunker lined out in black edged with straw. Valance straw lined. Black chimney, smokebox, footplate, tank tops, frames and other fittings below footplate. Inner edges of tyres and axle ends thinly lined in straw. Plain gilt and/or straw numbering on rear of bunker and lettering. Cast brass number plates on bunker sides, infilled with vermilion. Polished steel connecting and coupling rods, slide bars and valve gear, piston valve and cylinder cover plates, smokebox door hinges, fittings and handrails, buffer heads and shanks. Various bright brass fittings and connections.

District 'K' Stock 1927

After some two years of operation with 'G' class driving motor cars and mixed sets of early converted trailer cars, the District found a need both for extra rolling stock and for replacements for many of the older cars. A survey carried out in 1926 showed that at least 100 new cars were required, with over twice that number of new sets of traction equipments being needed to update older motor cars and those converted from trailers. Older converted trailers known as Class H had further converted cars added to their ranks, and the final fulfilment of new stock requirements included the conversion of a number of 'C', 'D' and 'E' stock trailers to motor cars. The intention was that all motor cars should permanently face either east or west. Consequently, they were numbered oddly and evenly respectively so as to aid identification. This resulted in an order for 101 new motor cars, all of which were to face east, being placed with BRCW, the specification including their being fitted out with BT-H electro-

magnetic control equipments and General Electric WT54B traction motors.

The appearance of the new motor cars was a great improvement compared with that of the previous 'G' motor cars, having rounded and downswept ends to the Monitor-style roof. Fewer main side lights provided larger individual areas of glass, with a reduced number of glazing bars and beading strips. The car ends were semi-flush, with rebated glass, and the marker lights were reduced in size and were grouped in a panel on the front off-side. Both the marker lights and the destination indicator mounted above them were controlled from within the cab, thus eliminating the unsightly external fittings seen on earlier stock. Two pairs of double sliding passenger doors were provided on each side, while the driver's and guard's doors were of the hinged type.

Left:
'K' stock motor car No 639 as new in 1928. With the nicely radiused roof-ends this stock offered a greatly improved appearance compared with the 'G' class cars. Whilst the body is scarlet with black waist rail and solebar, the door colour still poses a problem. Described on earlier stock as being 'lake' (along with fascia strip and solebars), an actual sample shows what could be 'lake' that has blackened with time, could equally be black that has turned a matt 'blackberry' colour. *(U5144)*

Below left:
'K' stock motor car No 4251, running in a 'Q' stock train around 1960, is seen operating on the District Line with assorted trailer cars of later stock. *F. G. Reynolds*

Above:
A typical 'Q' stock train, with a 'Q27' motor car leading. Little had changed since their construction apart from conversion to air door working, and the fitting of electro-pneumatic brakes and retardation control, the first set of which came into operation in November 1938. The livery since that time had been plain scarlet for the body and doors. Light grey, or later red oxide roof areas soon became dark grey. All from the solebar down was black, except for light grey shoebeams. Gilt lettering and numbering with a thin black outline was standard. *G. Kichenside*

Specification:

Largely all-steel construction. Monitor-style roof with louvred ventilation. Heavy plate frame 'A2' motor bogie fitted with GEC WT 54B traction motors and BT-H electro-magnetic control. Heavy plate frame 'K2' trailer bogie. All cars with Westinghouse brake and compressor. Double block rigged brakes.

Layout: Semi-open saloon form, seating 40 Third Class passengers, although two companion seats in the guard's compartment were available to the public when the latter was not in use.

Marshalling: Ran in sets of mixed stock comprising older motor and trailer cars, usually with an equal number of motors to trailers. Examples:

M-T-T-M-T-M-T-M
M-T-T-M-T-M.

Livery:

Initially retained the 1924 scheme of scarlet body, with crimson lake on doors only. Solebars, waist rail and all underframe equipment including bogies black. Light grey roof and shoebeams.

Stock numbering:

Builder	Year	District No
Birmingham	1927	499-699 odd numbers only

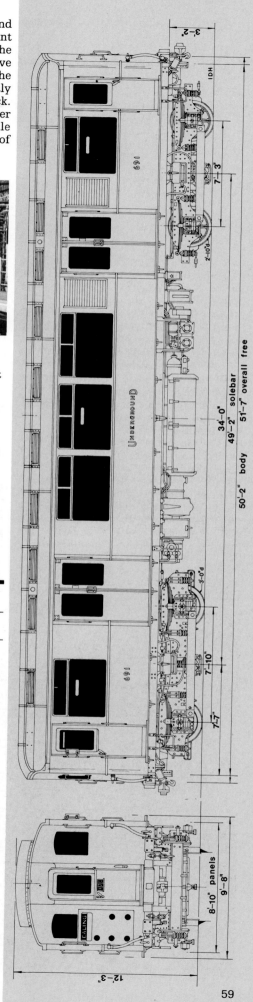

Metropolitan 'MW' Electric Stock 1926

With a rapid growth in traffic on the Extension Lines, and experience gained in the use of the experimental 1925 multiple-unit train, the MET management was faced with something of a dilemma in 1926 as to exactly what form the next generation of electric extension line stock should take. The most obvious answer was to revert back to the traditional compartment stock style of the steam era. However, a trial period using this type of stock was thought necessary so a new style of compartment stock motor car was designed. The new design was equipped in two different ways — one (later classed as 'MW' stock) fitted with buckeye couplings and Westinghouse brake equipment for hauling the 'Bogie' stock cars (previously propelled by 1905 motor cars) and the other (later classed as 'MV' stock) fitted with side buffers and standard vacuum braking for hauling the 'Dreadnought' steam stock.

The basic form of the new motor car combined the layout of the 1925 experimental motor cars — namely having all the control gear in a compartment between the driver and luggage area — and the multiple compartment layout of the 'Dreadnought' stock. There was sufficient space for five passenger compartments and a further one for the guard. Propulsion was achieved by the fitting of MET-VICK MV153 traction motors to heavy plate-and-angle bogies as used on the 1925 cars.

Six of each of both types of the new motor car were ordered from Met-Cam for delivery in 1927. In service they proved to be highly successful, and with ambitions of total electrification of the MET in mind, the 'MW' form was given priority for development as all equipments and couplings were compatible with the rest of the electric stock. Use of the 'Bogie' stock with the 'MW' motor cars was only of a temporary nature as future orders for similar motor cars would include matching trailer cars.

Below:
Apart from wider luggage compartment doors and the provision of only a single window in the guard's compartment, the side buffer and vacuum brake-equipped 'MV' driving motor car No 207, had an almost identical body style, with square-cornered beading, to that of the centre coupler and Westinghouse brake-equipped 'MW' driving motor cars. *(H/12229)*

Top:
1929 'MW' driving motor car No 2741 (formerly No 241) shows many differences over the earlier motor cars. The roof height is lowered over the switch compartment, so that larger cowled ventilators can be fitted. Beading on the driving end has been simplified, and on the sides the fascia board is incorporated with the panelling, all of which has radiused corners. Leaf springing is arranged in sets of three over each axlebox. *(2750)*

Above:
1931 'MW' stock followed a similar style but was flush panelled. Driving motor car No 2744 (formerly No 244) was originally grained and stippled over its metal panels to represent varnished teak. However, after 1945, as the whole fleet began to age, it was decided to overpaint them with a plain dark brown enamel, as they came up for overhaul. *L. Sandler*

Specification:

Steel underframe with composite floor structure. Hardwood framed body mainly wooden panelled with some steel panelling below the waistline. Double equipped, heavy plate-frame motor bogies with MV153 275hp traction motors — one per axle. MET-VICK electro-pneumatic control. Heavy duty, double block rigged brakes. Westinghouse brake and compressor.

Layout: Five Third Class compartments, seating 50 (five-a-side).

Marshalling: Initially two motor cars at either end of eight 'Bogie' vehicles. Later with five matching electric trailer coaches.

Stock numbering:

The 'MW' motor cars emerged first for trial service.

Builder	Year	Met No	LPTB No
Met-Cam	1927	200-205	2700-2705

Livery:

The initial livery comprised a clear varnished teak finish. To achieve this the wood panels were clear varnished, but the few lower steel panels were grained, stippled and varnished to represent the natural wood. Roof briefly white lead, changing to a silver-grey. White or ivory numbering and lettering with dropped blue shading. Gilt/straw lining. Solebars and all underframe gear dark grey, with light grey shoebeams.

In later years the roof area, which always deteriorated to a dull grey, was painted bauxite (which still turned full grey in time), whilst the main body was painted dark brown. Solebars and all underframe gear were painted black.

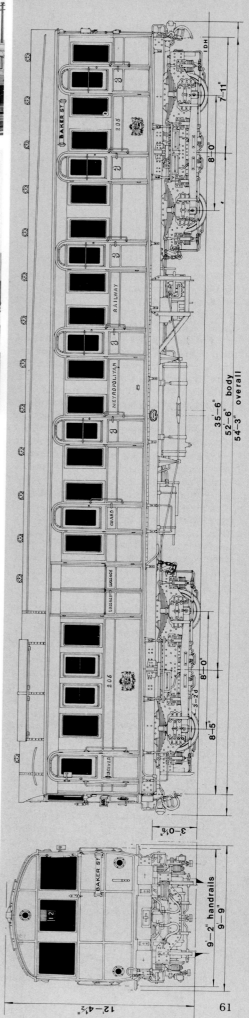

London Transport 'O' and 'P' Series Stock from 1937

The formation of London Transport (LPTB) with the complete amalgamation of the MET and MDR (and the tube lines of the LER) on 1 July 1933 brought about further efforts to standardise rolling stock where possible. Various new ideas in traction control were available, as well as the latest in car body styling, the latter resulting from changes in constructional methods.

New stock was urgently required for both the MET's Hammersmith & City line and the rest of its network (excepting the Aylesbury extension line). The District also required much additional stock, so in 1935 orders were placed with both Gloucester and BRCW for a whole series of cars designated 'O', 'P' and 'Q' respectively for the lines mentioned.

Basically a new design of car with an all-steel, flush exterior was developed, which served all three classes of stock. However, each was fitted out and equipped in quite different ways.

'O' STOCK: This was designed for the H&C, and had the guard's position shared within the driving compartment. Incorporating 'Metadyne' control equipment, the stock operated in basic two-car units, each car was the mirror image of the other with four of the eight axles powered.

'P' STOCK: Designed for the MET lines, this stock had a conventional guard's position in the end of a motor car, and here it is necessary to point out that with the 'Metadyne' equipment, two cars could be controlled from one driving position, via a single 'Metadyne' unit in one of the two cars. The 'Metadyne' involved no resistance banks so offered smooth acceleration, and regenerative braking.

Both 'O' and 'P' stock had automatic couplers which connected all pneumatic and electrical supplies in one single unit. Trains were formed into four-, six- or eight-car sets, which were soon found to be both lacking in operational flexibility and heavy on current consumption. Thus a number of 'O' and 'P' stock trailers were later

Above:
'O' stock driving motor car No 13029 as new, with scarlet body, silver-grey roof and black underframe gear with white tyre edges. This car contains the Metadyne equipment, and as delivered had no ventilation panel set into the driving end above the centre door. The date was 4 September 1937. *(U24346)*

constructed, enabling three-car units to be made up if required, giving rise to four-, five-, six-, seven- or eight-car trains. 'O' and 'P' stock equipments however were not interchangeable, even though coupling and control were compatible.

The trailer shells were identical to those of the motor cars, except that no driving compartment bulkhead was fitted and the 'driver's' doors were locked. Fitted out, the space contained two double seats. By that means, trailer cars could at any future time be converted into new motor cars.

'Q' STOCK: This was designed for use on the District lines, and was equipped to couple and run with older stock. The 'Metadyne' unit was replaced with resistance and contactor control equipments, and carried through bus-line power cable, together with the non-automatic coupler and external pneumatic and other electrical connections. Different traction motors were fitted. 'Q' stock trailer shells were identical to the 'O' and 'P' units.

'R' STOCK: Postwar versions of the 'O', 'P' and 'Q' classes entering first in service in 1949 and whereby all cars in a set were powered. The 'R' class can be sub-divided into four, 'R38', 'R47', 'R49' and 'R59'. They were constructed from 'Q' trailers rebuilt as 'R38' driving motor cars and newly-built 'R47' non-driving motor cars. 'R49' was similar stock but was of light-weight aluminium unit construction, driving, and non-driving motor cars. 'R59' stock comprised non-driving motor cars, of aluminium construction, with different external panelling left unpainted.

'CO/CP' STOCK: From 1955 some 17 'O/P' type trains were converted from 'Metadyne' to BT-H, PCM (pneumatic camshaft) control for the Circle Line, as the former equipment was becoming unreliable and costly to replace. From 1959 it was decided to convert all remaining 'O/P' stock over to PCM control. This programme started with the Hammersmith and City Line and went on to cover all MET main line stock.

Specification:

'OPQ' stock comprised steel underframe, and steel framed and panelled unit construction body. Heavy welded plate frame bogies having extra wide positioning of bolster springing and wing links, with an offset pivot. Motor and trailer bogies were identical save for the former having one powered axle. Dual braking was carried, one for motor bogies, the other for trailer bogies. Traction motors for 'O/P' stock with 'Metadyne' control were 152hp type MV145AZ.

'Q' stock with BT-H electro-magnetic control had WT54B type traction motors. Westinghouse brake and compressor. Double block rigged brakes. 'R49' and 'R59' stock employed aluminium integral frame and body and 110hp LT111, traction motors. The same motors also were fitted to R38 and R47 motor cars.

Layout: Semi-open saloon, giving 40 seats in all motor cars and 44 in trailer cars and with two extra companion seats. Third Class motors, First/Third, and Third Class trailers.

Marshalling: Initially in two motor car sets. Later with a trailer car. Then capable of various formations. 'Q' stock cars running with older stock in various formations also. 'R' stock in basic six-car sets and adding a further two-car set up to eight-car trains when required.

Stock numbering:

Original numbering for 'O', 'P' and 'Q' stock 1937-40.

Builder	Class	Type	'A' Car Nos	'D' Car Nos
Birmingham	O	M	13000- 13028	14000- 14028
Birmingham	P	M	13246- 13257	14246- 14257
Birmingham	P	1/3T	013258-013261	014258-014261
Birmingham	P	M	13262- 13269	14262- 14269
Birmingham	P	1/3T	013270-013273	014270-014273
Gloucester	O	M	13029- 13057	14029- 14057
Gloucester	O	3T	013058- 13077	014058-014076
Gloucester	O	1/3T	013078-013086	014077-014086
Gloucester	P	1/3T	013087-013101	014087-014100
Gloucester	Q	3T	013102-013104	014101-014103
Gloucester	Q	1/3T	013105-013166	014104-014166
Gloucester	Q	3T	013167-013192	014167-014192
Gloucester	P	M	13193- 13245	14193- 14245
Gloucester	Q	M	4402- 4420 (evens only)	4401- 4437 (odds only)

Conversion to 'CO' or 'CP' stock caused motor cars to be renumbered 5xxxx in place of 1xxxx ie: 13xxx and 14xxx become 53xxx and 54xxx.

From 1949, 'R' stock consisted of renumbered 'R38' driving motor cars (from 'Q' stock), together with newly-built cars, numbered in sequences following on from the motor cars. These were as follows:

Converted to driving motor cars as 'R38' vehicles (at Gloucester RCW and Acton LT Works): Nos 21100-21145, 21148-21150; 22600-22678 and 22683-22686.

'R47' new non-driving motor cars (89 built by BRCW, 54 by Gloucester RCW): Nos 23200-23230; 23300-23330; 23400-23430 and 23500-23549.

'R49' new driving motor cars (Met-Cam): Nos 21146-21147; 22679-22680 and 22681-22682.

'R49' new non-driving motor cars (Met-Cam): Nos 23231-23247; 23331-23347; 23431-23447 and 23550-23582.

'R59' new non-driving motor cars (Met-Cam): Nos 23248-23250; 23348-23350; 23448-23450 and 23583-23586.

Livery:

'O', 'P' and 'Q' stock took on the 1933-34 style of livery having plain scarlet body work, with black solebars and all below frame gear. The roof sheets between the car end curved roof panels was red oxide. Gilt numbering and lettering with thin black outline was applied to the body sides. Light grey shoebeams, and white tyre edges. 'R' stock followed the same style, until after the new aluminium stock had been in service for a while. After the trial use of an unpainted car, the stock then appeared with natural unpainted, non-reflecting alloy bodies having a narrow scarlet waistband. Gilt numbering with black outline was placed on the band. New scarlet lettering with black outline was used on the body sides. Dark grey roof sheets, and black solebars and all underframe gear. Light grey shoebeams and white tyre edges.

Steel motor cars were painted in a matching non-reflective silver-grey, and lined and lettered as the alloy cars. Later the scarlet waistband was removed.

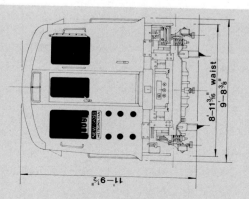

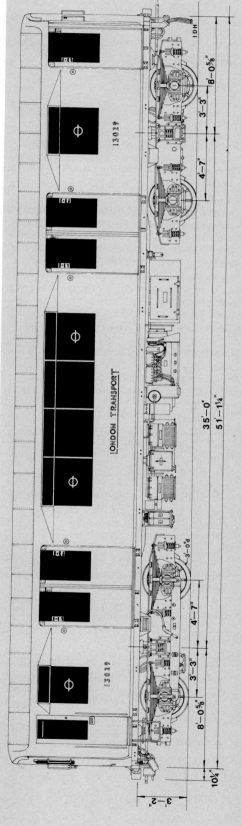

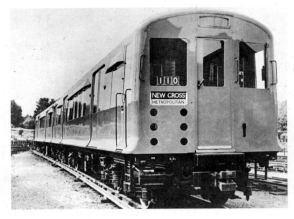

Above:
'O' stock train with driving motor car No 14029, showing a ventilator let into the end, above the centre door. The automatic coupler has been replaced with temporary coupling presumably for a delivery journey hauled by a steam locomotive and match wagon. *(4012)*

Above right:
'R38' driving motor car No 21150 painted silver-grey with a scarlet waistline to match unpainted aluminium 'R59' non-driving motor cars. These trains were designed to operate in either six- or eight-car formations. For this reason the trains were not particularly flexible, as each car had its own position in a set. A fault on one car would put the whole set out of operation. *(490-77)*

Appendix 1
The Four-Rail Electric Traction System

Picking up a supply current from an external source, presents problems for a moving railway vehicle fitted out with electric traction. The street tram managed it via a trolley contacting an overhead conductor, with the return current being passed back through the running rails. The tram could also pick up current from a conductor within a conduit placed below ground.

Both were simple systems, but not very efficient due to leakages to earth, which could cause serious drops in voltage, and stray currents could damage nearby electric cables and conduits such as gas and water, due to electrolysis.

For that reason the Board of Trade laid down a ruling that the voltage drop between any two points in a system, should not exceed seven volts. Also, electric power can be either a direct current, or an alternating current, and as far as the early underground railways of London were concerned, there could be many answers to electric traction.

It was therefore necessary for the MET and MDR to first arbitrate a common system before putting electrification into operation.

The final outcome was a direct current system, as already in operation in several US cities, but using two insulated conductors rather than one, so that the earth leakage would be reduced, thus minimising the voltage drop to that within the seven volt maxima.

From a passenger safety point of view it was decided not to repeat the four-rail system of the joint 1899 electrification experiment, but place the negative conductor in the centre of the running rails. That enabled the outside positive conductor to change sides when required. Thus at a station it could occupy the furthest position from the platform edge.

When it was decided to first electrify the Ealing and South Harrow branch of the MDR, which was opened to traffic on 28 June 1903, due consideration had

been given to the other associated Yerkes tube railways then under construction, so that a compromise set of dimensions could be established, which would suit both tube and surface tracks, even though the matter of inter-stock running was only a remote possibility.

The negative rail was placed in the centre of the running rails, with the top surface 1½in above the running rail level. The positive rail was placed outside the running rails with its vertical centre-line 16in from the gauge rail, with its contact surface 3in above the same level. These basic standards still apply today to LRT's four rail system, as used throughout the whole network.

A further advantage of this sytem, is that the insulated power and return rails leave the running rails free to be used for signalling and other control purposes, without fear of interference from traction currents.

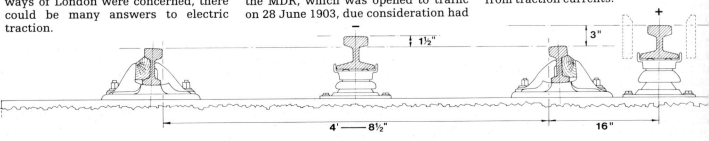